I Think I Can,
I Thought I Could,
I Did . . . I Will

I Think I Can,
I Thought I Could,
I Did . . . I Will

My Story

Katrina Roper-Smith

authorHOUSE®

AuthorHouse™
1663 Liberty Drive
Bloomington, IN 47403
www.authorhouse.com
Phone: 1-800-839-8640

First published by AuthorHouse   06/10/2011

ISBN: 978-1-4634-1004-9
ISBN: 978-1-4634-1003-2

Library of Congress Control Number: 2011909572

Printed in the United States of America

To my parents, Max and Mary Roper, for always being there; my two wonderful children, who have weathered the storms of life with me; Marion, a constant friend; and finally to my husband for his encouragement and belief in me and in this effort. To God be the glory for my story.

Introduction

So many times women are broken by the everyday toils of life. More often than not they are never able to put their lives back together again. My life was broken, torn, and ripped as though Hurricane Katrina had hit me personally. Every aspect of life at some point and time had been damaged. I thought I would never be able to mend the brokenness. My life challenges were more than I wanted to handle—until the day that I had an encounter with the potter and my thought process changed.

Like me, many women are confused about their journey. They question their existence, their purpose, and their place, and their lives seem doomed early on. There are scores of single mothers, teen mothers, divorced women, verbally and physically abused women, rape victims, addicted women, scorned women—and the list goes on. In the midst of these trails, they become directionally challenged and feel pulled in many dirction, thus locking them in the maze called life. Women look aimlessly, give graciously, yield to the unyielding, run ruthlessly, and race with the wind—simply to wind up right back where they started. How do we break this cycle and escape the maze of life with sanity, security, and self-worth? It starts with the thought process: we are what we think.

It is time for women to share their stories so that others can be healed. Across America women are hurting, damaged, and stuck in the maze. Some have experienced things that others will never imagine, unable to find their way to a place of peace. Through our stories, others can heal from their wounds and overcome obstacles, great and small. It is only when we begin to think of where we are and where we want to be that we can truly move forward; that's vision. Before you know it, you will say, "I thought I could"; that's reality. Soon you will realize that "I did"; that's accomplishment. Develop a personal relationship with God. and you will find yourself saying, "I will." There are no limits to what you can accomplish once you begin to say, "I will"; that's infinity.

PART I
I Think I Can

Chapter 1

The Beginning of Being an Outcast

Carter G. Woodson wrote in *The Mis-Education of the Negro,* "The 'educated negroes' have the attitude of contempt toward their own people because in their own as well as in their mixed schools Negros are taught to admire the Hebrews, the Greek, the Latin and the Teuton and to despise the African." P.1 [1] He also states that "the large majority of this class, then must go through life de-nouncing white people because they are trying to run away from the blacks and decrying the blacks because they are not white." How ironic is this, and how true is this statement? I grew up in the mid-sixties and early seventies, and my life during the earlier years was reflected in Woodson's theory.

When I began first grade, my elementary school was integrated. The building still stands some forty years later in the small town in which I was raised. The walls were an ugly yellow, the desks and tables were worn, and there were no Caucasians in my class. My mother and Mrs. Amanda J. Austin were the two minority teachers who taught all of the minority children. The two other teachers were Caucasians, and they taught all of the Caucasian students. I guess it was the school system's method of slowing integration. We did everything separately even though we were in the same hallway. I cannot remember ever seeing the inside of their classrooms or playing on the playground with any of the students in the Caucasian classes. It would not be until I was in third grade that I would be in a desegregated classroom.

Oddly enough, while growing up I was always separate but equal to someone. My family was quite different from other families at that time in my neighborhood. It would be years later that my neighborhood would become economically mixed. Everyone on the block was an educator, all teachers and principals except for my dad; he was the outcast. Daddy was a handsome, uneducated, hustling man married to a beautiful, educated lady. They were outcasts as the odd couple. I really do not remember my family fitting into the cliché as a small child. It wouldn't be until much later that the educated society would accept Daddy. However, this did not bother Daddy or Momma in the least. If it did bother them, I never knew. I am sure that his profession of choice during the time had a lot to do with their wariness.

People soon began to realize that even though Dad was not educated, he was a swift and creative man with a great business sense. Dad had money to loan when everyone else was broke. He refused to work for anyone; he had held a job at the local paper mill when I was very young, but not for too long. Dad had a mind of his own and was determined to have a good life. Today, Dad still has a mind of his own and is still an entrepreneur.

What seemed normal for other children in my neighborhood was not exactly normal for me. As a child and teenager, I became an outcast in many ways. I had an educated mom and an uneducated dad, and truly it was just like Mr. Woodson described: many of those who worked with Mom in the earlier years decried the uneducated African Americans. The churches were even segregated by economical class. So, here I was with parents that were educationally opposites, and my dilemma soon became, "Where do I fit into this world?" I was not accepted by the children of uneducated parents because my mom was a teacher, and I was not really accepted by the students of educated parents because my dad was uneducated. Now as an adult, I am aware of the discussions that were taking place within the homes of my peers. Mom knew it then; Since I have become an adult, we have had many conversations about the hardships she went through during those years she was an outcast because of her marriage.

Soon I became the youngest outcast in the Roper family. In kindergarten, I was sent to a private school in the neighboring town, whereas most other kids in my town stayed home or with a relative. Kindergarten was a wonderful experience for me, and I met lifelong friends from the town of Greenville, Alabama. Like me they were all children of educated minorities.

Once I got to first grade, students began to make fun of me because I was the child of a teacher—a teacher who happened to be a first-grade teacher—and even though I was not in Mom's classroom, I was never able to forget that she was close by. Students did not let me live it down, and neither did my teacher. In kindergarten, the majority was children of teachers, and no one cared. The real world hit hard and heavy in first grade, and thus I received my first dose of being an outcast. As the elementary years rolled on, I found that more and more of the students made fun of me because I was the child of a teacher. My own race was the worst; I really was not accepted during my early school years, and unfortunately, none of my classmates' moms were school teachers. Somehow, everyone else who had teacher parents were older or younger. Most of the minority students did not accept me because of the stigma of being a teacher's daughter, and the Caucasian students did not accept me because I was a minority.

It was not until the middle grades that I began to find acceptance from minority peers, but I only found this acceptance by acting out and becoming somewhat rebellious. I tried anything and everything to fit in, including not doing my work, walking to schools with certain students, smoking, and even trying drugs. I just wanted to fit somewhere, and I wanted to please my parents at the same time.

Sadly enough, this is still going on today. Teens across the nation are still struggle with identity issues asking the question, "Who am I, and where do I fit in society?" Many are trapped like I was because of the same issues. Children today are still faced with segregation based on economic issues, preconceived notions, family reputations . . . the list goes on and on. I had the opportunity to minister to a student whose father was a minister. I was actually suspending her from school for the remainder of the year because of her behavior. The student had been dared by other students and decided to take up the dare. This is a subtle reminder that students are still faced with identity issues, and it also serves as a reminder of how cruel children can be to each other. As her mom sat in my office crying and telling her daughter how disappointed she was in her, I saw a reflection of myself and thousands of other children who were struggling to find their place in this cruel world as teenagers. Let it be known that low socioeconomic students are in no way the only students at risk.

My third—and fourth-grade experiences were totally desegregated. I remember the first time the partition was opened and the classes were joined. We were amazed—we loved having classes together! It was also the first opportunity for us to see the teachers interact with one another; team teaching in the experimental stages is what I like to call it now. The classes and teachers were racially mixed, and I gained many Caucasian friends during that time. Now, it is obvious that they were equal in socioeconomic status with my family, and no doubt they had been told with whom to socialize. However, by the seventh grade I lost many of those friends to the new private schools. Eighth grade and ninth grade brought on my first real acceptance experience. By that time, schools were totally desegregated, and no one cared anymore about my mom teaching. I had proven my point in my mind and was doing everything they were—everything that was good, bad, and ugly—but I still managed to keep good grades. Mom and Dad really did not hound me about making straight As, so I had some wiggle room.

Chapter 2
The Outcast Continues

By the eleventh grade life as I knew it would be no more. I had become the drum majorette for the Marching Georgiana High School Panthers. Previously I was the only African American majorette on a squad of four. Every week, Mom was making a new drum majorette suit; for some reason, they kept getting tighter and tighter. I was excited to be a drum majorette because it had been a battle to win the spot. I was told that I won by only a few points. The other young lady who competed would become my assistant. It was the first time in history that there would be an assistant drum major in this band. Of course, I had my reasons for suspecting her appointment, but that doesn't matter anymore. I now know that God has a plan in place for everything, and the girl's appointment was a part of His plan. I also know that sometimes we don't understand the plan.

I surely did not understand the plan for my life at that time. I was a slightly above average student. It was necessary for me to study hard because nothing came easy or natural, but I managed to do pretty well. As a slightly above average student, I became a member of the National Honor Society, band, chorus, and student council. As with most "successful" students, I was involved in distinguished organizations in high school. But none of this compared to my high school love, Terry. I had one of the catches of the school. He had graduated and gone to the army. My life would be filled with letters, calls, and a longing to be with him. After all, we had been an item for few years at this point.

My courtship would be that no different from any other teenager's. When Mom and Dad said no, I was determined to say yes, even if it meant sneaking, and that I did until the day the neighbor on the corner told on me in my eighth-grade year. We were crazy in love. Somewhere in all of the craziness and during his visits home after basic training, I became pregnant, and that is where I will pick up with "The Plan."

I did not actually know whether or not I was pregnant. I vividly remember lying on my bed to see if my stomach would go back to flat. The discussion of sex never came up in my house, and pregnancy never was discussed, not even for the "birds and the bees" talk. I knew by all accounts that something was wrong. I remember like it was yesterday. My mom was teaching kindergarten, and my granny and I had traveled to Evergreen, Alabama, to the doctor's office. I thought maybe it was just a bladder infection, but the doctor's gloomy and disappointed expression when he entered my examination room told me otherwise. He knew my family well, so I don't know if he was hurt because he knew my family, was disappointed in my age, or simply hated having to tell a fifteen-year-old that she was pregnant. When he told me, I broke into tears. My entire life was shattered. How would I ever tell Momma? Even worse, how and who would tell Daddy? He would kill Terry and me.

As I left the examination area, I immediately had to face Grandma, and if you knew my Grandma, you would understand that no one wanted to face Big Granny. But somehow, she already knew what was wrong. She always did. She told me on the way home. It would be a long trip down Interstate 65 south, and Grandma fumed the entire way home. I knew beyond a shadow of doubt that she was disappointed.

Grandma made me stop at the elementary school and tell Momma. That was one of the hardest things that I ever had to do. She cried and cried there in the parking lot of the school. I thought it was the end of the world.

Plans were made immediately to send me to Pensacola to live with my aunt and have the baby. This was a tough time for Momma. I never had a doubt that I would have the baby; her conviction in God was too strong. But I was sure all of her educated friends were telling her to make me have an abortion. I was a disgrace to the professionals in this small community. The feeling of being an outcast returned and would last for years.

After Christmas, I was sent to Pensacola, where I was enrolled at Washington High School and sent to Judy Andrews School for the Pregnant and Mentally Retarded. Yes, I rode the little short bus everyday with all pregnant teenagers. It would be a humbling experience. Again I felt like an outcast. From the socioeconomical aspect, I didn't fit in; from the educational aspect, I didn't fit in. The only thing that resembled the other girls on the bus was the color of my skin. One would think there would be a common bond because we were all pregnant, however, the standards for success and moral values that I knew so well were quite different from the other girls. I met girls who only knew dropping out of high school, living in the government housing, and receiving public assistance. This was foreign to me and never had crossed my mind as an option. I had simply made a mistake. Never once, while riding the bus, did I hear the other girls mention returning to school or having a career. But for me, I could not wait to return to school and get back to my normal routine. Little did I know—what had been normal would be no more. My life at the school during my pregnancy was so different. I had one special teacher who took time to explain child birth, career choices, and basic homemaking skills to me with such love and passion. I learned to care for my unborn child, cook, clean, clip coupons, and sew in a few short months from this special woman. Toward the end of my school year, the principal called me in along with my teacher and asked if I wanted to complete my courses and take the Florida's high school exit exam and finish school a year early. My grades were well above average and I was completing assignments at a quicker and more accurate pace than the other students. I declined the offer; for me, returning to my friends and graduating with my class was what I really wanted.

My family was supportive, and so was my soon-to-be husband. He was wonderful, coming to visit as often as possible, and he was excited by the baby. He immediately wanted to get married. Mom and Dad were coming every weekend, and I was growing daily. Life for those five months was quite different. I spent a lot of time watching, wrestling, and eating. Like everything else in my life, it would be one of the many tests of my inner strength, and now it is a testimony: twenty-six years later, I would return to Pensacola to tell my story to young ladies in the hopes that they would make better choices.

On August 15, 1981, I was married. It was a grand celebration, a beautiful but simple, outdoor summer wedding. Momma made all of the dresses, including my powder blue wedding dress. The groom was stunning in his matching tux. I immediately wanted to start traveling with him. However, we agreed that I would return to Georgiana High School and graduate. I was eager to return to school, but it would not take long for the outcast feeling to return. I was married, had a baby, and was only in the twelfth grade, but it was an awful experience. School was not the same; I was treated like I had the plague by teachers and students. I couldn't participate in the band (my favorite activity), and I was no longer a member of the honor society even though I transferred all As from Pensacola. If I took the baby to the doctor, it was counted as unexcused absence. The principal was a short, stocky man with a loud, deep voice. I can hear his voice as though it was yesterday. He saw my transcript and asked me, "How did you make all As there?" as if he thought the records had been fabricated. I remember my economic and government teacher telling me that I did not belong in school if I was married and with a baby. It is hard to forget the feeling of not being able to participate in the band. All of these unpleasant memories were the factors that drove me to say, "I can." They were all constantly telling me that I could not, and I wanted to prove them wrong.

By December of 1981, I had had enough of school, teachers, and the educational system. All I wanted was to go with my husband and forget the rest. Dad evidently was tired of the school system, too, and he agreed with my quitting school. I quit and immediately went to the local junior college to take my GED.

The first glimmer of hope was restored when I walked out of the test, and the lady administered the test said, "You must have thought it was easy." I passed with a high score. I was very proud of myself, and although others would talk about how a GED was not equal to a high school diploma, I always knew that my knowledge from my high school experiences and life experiences could not be measured in such simple terms. I had gained more in my high school years than many would gain in a lifetime—that could not be measured by a simple paper test. Life had taught me many lessons that would have never been learned in the course of four years of high school. My education was just beginning.

Chapter 3

Growing Up

When I was a child, I spoke as a child, I
understood as a child, I thought as a child;
but when I became a man, I put away childish
things.

—1 Corinthians 13:11

In January 1982, I found myself traveling abroad.
My husband had been sent to Germany, stationed in
Kaiserslaugen, and I soon flew to be with him. I went to
Kaulser and stayed with a neighbor from home. I would
babysit during the week and wait fervently for my spouse
to come on the weekends. It was not long before he had
found us a place to live in "K-town," as they called it. It was
a cozy, one-bedroom apartment with three rooms total. The
shower was in the kitchen, we shared a toilet with a German
wino, and life was great. We were happy and happily in
love; things were simple. It would be during this time that I
learned to drive a stick shift VW bug, our first car together.
It would also be during this time that I would have my first
car accident.

We savored each moment that we were together, and our marriage was wonderful. We were broke by the end of each month and counted change to make it to payday. We cashed in the few savings bonds that we had until that soon ran out, so we walked and rode the train to get where we needed to go. Washing clothes meant packing the duffle bags, walking to the train station (with the clothes, mind you), riding across town to the Laundromat, and going back again. Times were hard, and we longed to live on post and for my husband to get the rank of E-4. The rank of E-4 for those in the army meant we now had the option of living on the base housing without the worries of monthly expenses. It also meant having a washer and dryer, other Americans nearby, and easy access to everything on base verses riding the bus. But life was also good, and we were happy.

That is what I remember most about this time in my life and life with husband one: with him, simple meant life was always better. The love of money was one of the roots of evil in our marriage. Mom and Dad had agreed to keep Talarrius, our child, and so it was like an extended honeymoon.

Even though we were happy, it didn't take long for me to realize that I needed more that a GED to help make it in the real world. After searching and searching for a job, I realized that we were going to need more than just one income. To his credit, my husband at the time was always good about taking care of his responsibilities. I must give him his just dues; he didn't waste money that I knew of, nor did he ever try to hide anything. He was ideal in every sense of the word as a husband during those simple times in our lives.

It would not take long for our lives to change, however. The outside world invaded our simple lifestyle. We moved into housing on base, and that was the end of my naïve life. The things I learned and saw . . . Trust me, it is another world, the military life. You either fit or you do not, and for me, I had to do a lot to fit in. I was introduced to the club scene, to adulterous affairs, drugs, drinking, weekend cookouts, and competition among wives—and the root of all evil in each case was money. Everyone wanted rank, all wives wanted to work the high-paying jobs, and there were certain expectations that went with traveling abroad. Everyone had to have conversational pieces. As I think back on that time in my life, although I did not take up traveling to other parts of Europe as many others did, I fell into the competitive atmosphere. I worked hard and so did he in an effort that we could buy things that everybody else had. We had to have the all important crystal from Germany, the china, the cuckoo clock, the furniture, and the stereo. What we had before, a simple life where we trusted and depended on each other, would soon go out of the door. I worked at the mess hall, and together we made pretty good money for as young as we were. I began to feel the peer pressure from other wives and wanted so badly to fit in. I did a lot of which I am quite ashamed.

We would occasionally go to church while in Germany, and for us that was not normal. After all, as kids back home, we were in church all of the time; we went to church together before we were married. It was after the pregnancy and during this time in our lives that we forgot all about what we knew to be right and wrong. It would not take long for God to show up and remind me that I had abandoned His ways and the way I was brought up. My heart ached and my conscience was very alert to my wrong doings. I knew deep within that I was too far out—and when I say too far out, my definition of far out and someone else's maybe totally different. We were not doing what many were doing; we were just not doing as we had been raised to do, having strayed off course. We were following the crowd, and deep down I knew we were wrong.

At eighteen, I had done more and seen more of life than I cared too. Now that I look back on life, while others my age would be in college, still depending on parents and enjoying the college life, I was being a full-time parent, working full-time, gaining responsibilities, and learning about life the hard and dirty way. Most of all, every day I was competing with the army for my husband, and he was competing with the army for me. We both were forced to grow up.

God would use this time in my life to reintroduce Himself to me. I sat in our bedroom on a golden-winged chair and prayed for deliverance. I can see still myself sitting on the arm of the chair crying and asking God to deliver me from the mess that I was making out of my life. I didn't know how He would, but I was hoping that He would. This was also be the first time that God would show me that He answered prayers, but maybe not in the manner in which I though. I went to the doctor a few days later and discovered that I was pregnant with our second child, Quenita. The doctor said that I could not deliver the baby in Germany because of the possible risk involved. My first child had been delivered by C-section and had minor health issues that caused him to stay in the hospital for weeks after I was dismissed. It is funny now that I reflect upon the discussion with the doctors; they never provided me with a reason as to why I could not deliver the child in Germany. To me this was God's way of delivering me from the circumstances and situation. I realize now that it should have been possible to deliver the baby there. Thus I found myself traveling back to Alabama with Talarrius to deliver Quenita.

Once I returned to Alabama, I was angry with the world. Even though I didn't want to remain in that situation in Germany, I did not want to go home. I sure did not want to hear Momma talk about church or to follow her around to church. I was a grown woman and did not need her telling me where to go and what to do. Yes, I wanted God to deliver me from my mess—but then I wanted to forget He existed. It would take years and years before I would tell about my prayer on the back of the chair that day.

Momma would not give up, and God did not give up either. I went with her to church against my wishes. She was so patient. The more I went, the more I would see God and feel His presence, and the more I would realize that God truly did exist. It would be through following Momma and two adoptive aunts that I was truly introduced to God, to studying God's word, to conventions, to other people working for God, and most important to my blessing—a blessing that would pick me up at my lowest point in life and instill in me the true concept of "You can."

I followed them everywhere. Both aunts were related to me in some way; they were not technically my aunts, but adult relatives that were on the circuit for God. I learned more about the church in those few years than I ever thought I could. I would attend classes and the Easion Baptist Seminary, Greenville extension weekly; I would go to every possible workshop and class offered through the church. I quickly begin to realize that I had just as much fun in the church as I did in the world, and I did not feel like an outcast even though I was the youngest in the bunch. I was having the time of my life in church;

I was safe and secure. These years brought on growth in all aspects of my life. Most important, it was my birth in Christ.

Chapter 4

A Place to Belong

To every thing there is a season, and a time to
every purpose under the heaven.
—Ecclesiastes 3:1

Quenita was born, her father was home, and I was quite confused about what I wanted in life. I had experienced both sides of living, knowing what each had to offer. After the birth of Quenita, he returned to Germany and I remained in Georgiana. I immediately got a job at McDonald's. I worked long and hard hours but had fun. It was a unique experience, and I made many new friends. One of those was a handsome man who was a quiet, soft-spoken gentleman, and he never went out of his way to harm a fly. He had the patience of Job and a sweet spirit. Thanks to him and a wonderful nightshift manager, I learned as much as I could about the operations and learned how to work everything in the place. We would work hard during the day shift, but my favorite shift was night. There were five regular closers; everyone on the night shift quickly became good friends, and it was the first time I truly began to grasp the concept of teamwork. We did everything together at work and after work; a few even got married to each other. I finally had a place to belong and loved every moment of it.

A great friend, the same friend that had taught me true meaning of "You can," also said to me, "Katrina, if you must settle for working in McDonald's, at least be the best hamburger flipper there." I have kept that attitude in life: in everything that I do, I strive to be the best. This thought is always in my mind, and I never deviate from it.

In addition to working at McDonald's, I had fallen in love with the church. I was traveling across the country, going to meetings, revivals, and conventions at the local, state, and national level. I had found another place where I belonged. I made friends with young ladies from across the state of Alabama and from other parts of the United States who were just like me. They did not care that I was young with two children. Soon I was working in the New Era Baptist State Convention in the Junior Women Auxiliary, traveling with the convention and having a ball. Three of us became known as the Radical Junior Women from Alabama. We did not mind; we loved the Lord and were not ashamed to tell the world.

I was learning more and more about God's word and enjoying it. God had proved Himself to me once, but now His word was being drilled in my heart, becoming a light unto my path. I was able to carry the children and learn about God all at the same time. I was accepted for being a child of the king. I found a place to belong, a place in God's kingdom among God's people. Life has never been the same since I accepted God in my life. It is something about a true encounter with the Almighty that never allows one's life to be the same. Somehow, some way, God has a way of bringing His children back into his fold. That would happen to me soon.

Things in the marriage were not great. We were experiencing some difficult times upon my husband's return home. I had changed my lifestyle and friends, I was working and making my own money, and things were different. We did not see eye to eye on anything, and we both had made some serious mistakes. I had found the freedom of not only the church and work, but the freedom to come and go as I please. This was a freedom that I had never experienced going from Mom and Dad's house to his house. I was enjoying my newfound freedom, hanging out with my friends and everything that went with it.

The army had delivered orders for him to be stationed in Fort Rucker, Alabama, close to our home town. I did not want to move and give up my place of belonging, only to return to being an outcast. I had a family now. I refused to deal with the problems, so I left. I left the children with Mom and Dad and returned to Pensacola. I moved back in with my aunt and soon got a job at a local trucking company. I had no experience as a secretary other than working with Daddy in the vault company. I had only worked at McDonald's in Greenville and at the mess hall in Germany, but I was excited about this job. It was an opportunity for me to have a more prestigious job. I was going to be a secretary; I really thought I was moving up in the world.

This experience would turn out to be one that I would not forget. It was fun, and my cousins and I ventured into many different things—one being a decision not to go to our traditional Baptist church. Somehow we found a little church in the back of a house. A small, middle-aged lady was the pastor. This was the first time that I had experienced a female as a pastor, and it was also my first experience with people dancing in church, speaking in tongues, laying of hands, and using anointing oil. Boy, was our family mad with us, but we were all trying to find and develop in the Lord, and we wanted to do it our way. We refused to listen to anything that any of the older adults had to say about where we went to church. We did not miss a single service held at the church. It was quite a different experience, but it didn't last that long; neither did my tour of duty in Pensacola.

God would once again show up very vividly in my life, the second of such dramatic experiences. This time was even more profound than the experience in Germany. The children's father's leave was up, and he was in Fort Rucker, Alabama. I was torn between staying in Pensacola or going back and trying to work things out. I moved out of the house with my aunt and for the first time had my own apartment, my own job, and a taste of freedom. I did not have the children and was really living the life of a single person. Life was quite different and I was enjoying it. But deep down inside, once again I knew I was living a life not pleasing to God. I did not have my children, I was not divorced from my husband, I was attempting to date other men, and I was going contrary to all of the teachings of the past two years while hanging with Mom and my aunts. Everything in me was telling me that I was wrong.

I was actually dating the preacher's son. Even though he did not attend church, somehow he had managed to catch my eye and I his. He was very unique, in my opinion, and was determined not to listen to his mother or attend church. He was tall, thin, and dark, and he had a pleasing personality. He was fun to be around, yet he seemed sheltered. He worked every day and would visit me at night. One morning a knock came on my door. It was my aunt, and she stormed into my apartment like a mighty rushing wind. "Where is he? I know he is staying with you." She was dressed for work in her scrub uniform; she worked at one of the local hospitals, in the cafeteria. She proceeded to tell me that I was living wrong, that I should be ashamed of myself, and that I needed to pack my things and move back to my husband and kids.

I knew deep down inside she was right. I felt like a total failure at that point. Again I found myself in an odd place and going to the Lord in prayer for a way out of the mess. Even though I had found my place of belonging in Christ, I was still just a babe who was not really sure of what God was capable of doing. My support system that I had gained in the previous year was no longer there; I was on my own, just me and God. I prayed and asked Him for directions. "God, if it is your will that I go back to my husband, then you close my job, and I will know what to do." As far as I knew, nothing had been said about closing down the trucking company; business was good, and there was nothing to indicate that my job might be in jeopardy. I was really pushing it with God now. Who did I think that I was, giving God an ultimatum? Reflecting back on that prayer, I was really doubting God and asking him to do what I thought was impossible, not really understanding at that moment that nothing was impossible with God.

I went to work that morning, and everything was business as usually. We always went out for lunch. Upon returning from lunch, the boss said, "Katrina, we are closing the company. You have the option of staying to the end of the day or leaving now." I immediately said I was leaving. What else was there for me to say? God had showed up and showed out. I could not doubt what was going on or even second guess what to do. If God did this, in my mind, He was telling me what to do and to do it now. I went to the apartment, called home, and told them to come and get me and my things. I was going to Fort Rucker. Mom and my husband were there by late afternoon. I didn't bother to break the lease, read the agreement, or pay anything—I just left.

This would be the second of many profound experiences with God. I never second guessed moving. I never looked back at Pensacola, I never said good-bye. I left Pensacola on that evening with my husband, mother, and children. He had found a house on base, and we were soon on our way to Fort Rucker.

Fort Rucker was good for the two of us. After a while mending our marriage, we were able to travel to Georgiana on the weekends to church. We were back where we had started in church, back in the place and security that we knew. His gift was singing, and the pastor had put me back playing the piano. Earlier in our teenage years, we were a duo. He had a voice like no other, and he never complained or had anything bad to say about my playing. I was not that good, but he made me sound good. We enjoyed our time in church, following the congregation everywhere singing and playing. My spouse became a deacon during this time, and that made me so very proud of him. Life was good: we had returned to a simple life of dedication to the Lord and to each other. We both traveled to conventions and soaked in as much as possible about God's word.

During this time, I worked as an assistant manager at Cato's and later became a secretary at Mars White Knight Textiles in Ozark, Alabama. My plant manager at Mars White Knight gave me my glimmer of hope in completing a post-secondary education. Both Terry and I were taking classes, but I was provided with an opportunity to go to classes during my lunch hour and return to work after class. I worked hard during the day and even did overtime so that I could attend classes. I was proud of myself. I completed my computer certification course from Wallace State Junior College.

We stayed in Fort Rucker for three years. Then can the orders to return to Germany. I was devastated. We had good friends who went to church with us, I had a great job that I enjoyed, the children were stable, and I enjoyed my home. I did not want to return to the life that I once knew in Germany.

Chapter 5

A Prayer Answering God

Hear my Cry O God; attend unto my prayer,
From the end of the earth will I cry unto thee,
when my heart is overwhelmed; lead me to the
rock that is higher than I. For thou hast been
a shelter for me, and a strong tower from the
enemy.

—Psalms 61:1-3

I guess I was like David in the Psalms. I really did not want to go back to Germany, however Terry was adamant about his family going with him instead of traveling later, so all four of us were off to Europe once again. I prayed and prayed, sure that if God could pull a rabbit out of His hat one time, then He could do it again. I reverted back to the Pensacola prayer days. I started praying all kinds of "if, then" prayers. "Lord, if it is your will that I go back, then . . ." I guess I just knew that God would not send us back. Oddly enough, every time I would give God an "if, then" statement, He would do the then. For example, I would try stuff like, "God, if it is your will for me to go back to Germany, then let us sell this car." We did not sell the car. Can you imagine little ole me trying God like that? Some of you are probably trying Him right now. Do not do it; Just ask Him for what you want and be ready to accept the answer. I was not ready for my answer.

Big Granny was sick with Alzheimer's during this time. My first cousin was a teenager and was staying with her; she had spent many summers with us at Fort Rucker babysitting and was pretty good at it, so staying with Granny was not hard. The disease was pretty bad, but we were not really familiar with it, and the treatment was not nearly as good as it is now. Big Granny's condition was progressing quickly. As with many grannies, she was the pillar of the family. Granddaddy had been dead for about ten years. I spent as much time as possible with Granny between the Fort Rucker move and the trip to Germany.

Big Granny stayed with us on the night before we left for Germany. My cousin was not getting much sleep because of Granny walking throughout the night, so Mom talked Big Granny into staying at our house as much as possible. I had a talk with Granny and told her to stay until I returned from Germany. I told her not to die, but to be there when I returned.

We were in Germany for all of two weeks when the call came: Big Granny had passed away. This was the second of such deaths while I was in Germany; My mom's oldest sister, Aunt Bessie, who had been instrumental in my life, had passed during my first trip. Immediately I returned to the States and arrived just in time to attend the funeral. I kept telling myself, "I told her to wait until I got back."

Why was this important? Well, somewhere in my experience of praying, I asked God not to send us to Germany. I expressed my interest in not going and gave

Him several "if, then" statements to determine my stance on the trip. I truly believe that God answered my prayers several times, but I did not know how to receive His answer. I was looking for an answer with fanfare like that which I received in Pensacola. Now I know that God does answer prayers; however, we must open our minds to receive the answer even if answer is not what we want to hear.

God gave me directions and a clear answer to my question about returning to Germany. Nothing, absolutely nothing, fell in place for us once we got to Germany. This trip would have us stationed miles away from Frankfort, with nowhere for the children and me to live. The housing had been mixed up, and we had no place to stay. Once again we would wait until he returned on the weekends. Our orders were wrong, and nothing went right on that trip. Oddly enough, although I know it was Big Granny's time to go, because God already numbered everyone's days, I believe that Granny's death was God's way of bringing me back to Georgiana and to the life that was prepared for me by Him.

Once I returned to Alabama, I decided to stay. This decision was not mutually agreed upon by Terry and I. Right or wrong, I made the decision without consulting God. Talarrius was in the third grade and had been enrolled in school at Fort Rucker, at Ozark, at Germany, and now at Greenville. That was too much to ask a child to adjust to. I wanted to stay until he completed the third grade, but Terry would not hear of that. We constantly disagreed on that point. He wanted us to return immediately; he was a stickler for his family being together. Although I was probably a little selfish, I wanted to be close to Mom, Dad, and the life that I had grown to love and feel comfortable in. I never wanted to give it up and return to Germany, so I stayed.

I immediately returned to school, enrolling at the local junior college where I had received my GED, and I was well on my way somewhere. I did not have a clue about what I wanted to do or be. I had the computer background, but it would not take long for me to realize that there was a major difference between a technical school and junior college. My credits from the technical college did not transfer.

Terry summoned me to return to Germany by the end of that school year, and I was confused about what to do. He had a promising future in the army and loved his career. I had nothing—two children, seven years of marriage, no retirement fund, no future, and nothing to look forward to. My independence had kicked in, but I loved my husband with all that was in me, and I wanted more than anything to be with him once I completed my education. We both were stubborn. What was a girl to do?

I was very confused. I was enjoying school and learning a lot. Everyone I knew was in college—at least, that is how it appeared to me. Another one of my many cousins was attending AUM, and I stopped by to take her something while I was going to Montgomery. I remember as though it was yesterday how God answered my prayer. This was His fourth direct and profound example of His ability to make things plain and clear to me. I was walking across the campus of AUM after seeing my cousin, just strolling along during a beautiful summer day. The campus was in full bloom. It was a fairly new campus, and everyone was excited about the new extension. Everything around me was fresh and new, and it was like God was showing me a new and fresh life. The air was crisp, and I can remember looking toward Heaven and smiling as I walked across the campus. Somehow, at that moment I felt like I did not have a care in the world. A feeling like none other came over me, one that I can't explain and that I have not forgotten. As I walked from the dorm room back to my car, I heard His voice say, "This is what you are supposed to do." I knew at that moment that I would not be returning to Germany, but rather I would be attending school full time until I completed my degree. I thought, "I think I can."

My prayers this time were answered in unexpected ways, yet God proved once again that He was in control and that He was a prayer-answering God. My pathway was cleared, and there was no doubt about the direction in which I was to take. It appears as though I lost a lot to get to the beginning of where I am now, but His ways are not our ways, and His thoughts are not our thoughts.

PART II
I Thought I Could

Chapter 5
The Lost Sheep

All we like sheep have gone astray; we have
turned every one to his own way; and the Lord
hath laid on him the iniquity of us all.
—Isaiah 53:6

I was determined to not live in a house with Mom
and Dad and to do my own thing, so I moved in the little
house up the street. I was getting a divorce. A difference
in career choices, time, and distance had driven us apart.
Both parties, however, were not in full agreement with the
divorce. Terry still wanted us to return to Germany; I, on
the other hand, was more determined than ever to finish
school. In the midst of all of this determination, I lost my
way.

I moved into the small, three-bedroom house on the
corner of Morgan Street and Peagler Avenue in Georgiana.
This was the same house that I had met my husband at
every morning so that we could walk to school together,
just a few years earlier. The owner of the house was the
one who enlightened my parents about my premature

relationship with my future husband. Now I was moving in her house without him. The house was worn by the years. The floor was warped from the unstable seals underneath, and it reeked of snitch from the previous tenants. There were holes in the walls that were concealed with furniture, and it had cracks from the lack of basic maintenance. But it did not matter; I moved my furniture in and made the best out of the situation. At least I did not have to share the bathroom.

The years to follow would be trying years. Three hundred fifty-eight dollars per month in food stamps, three hundred dollars per month in child support, and forty dollars per week for gas from Dad—that was my total income per month. Dad had always said, "You've made your bed hard; now lie in it." He told me that he would help with the children and provide me with gas to make it to and from school, but that was all. He stuck to that. Somehow it seemed as though he knew exactly how much gas it would take to make it to Troy and back daily. He would give me the forty dollars every Sunday as if he was giving me my allowance. The rest was up to me.

I worked at a night club to pick up extra money, although it was against everything that I had been taught. I allowed a man to move in, thinking that it would help somehow. It seemed as though all of God's revealing of His power went out of the window again. I really do not know what I was thinking. I stopped going to church, hung out at the clubs, pushed the children on my parents, and went into another negative world. Though it was not quite as bad as it was in Germany, I experienced things during those years that I never wish to experience again.

During this time I was introduced to domestic violence. My live-in friend and I would fight almost every weekend.

This was something that I had never done or seen before. Certainly my parents did not fight in my presence; even though I knew they did argue, it was always well hidden from my little ears. He was fine Monday through Thursday, but after Thursday it was another story. Like clockwork, that day he would start drinking and would continue consistently through Saturday. He was at best a weekend alcoholic. This time was not spent with me, but rather at the local shot houses and wherever else he could find beer and liquor. His entire personality would change.

The best that I know, at least three children were conceived with three different women during his stay with me. Each case he had an excuse for his actions, but the women did not mind confronting me and making it known that they were pregnant with his child. I even became bold enough to go look for him out of desperation and a determination not to be out done by the other women. That did not work; he did not care nor did the women. He was simply making a mockery of me. Soon most things that were breakable in the house had been broken and super glued at least once. I was known for picking up anything to hit him with it. I make no excuses for what happened; it was a terrible living atmosphere and one that I do not recommend.

To date, I don't know who received the most damage, me or him. If anything, my ego was greatly damaged. It was particularly embarrassing when the local pastor came to the house, knocked on the door, and proceeded to tell me about my lifestyle, about which he had learned from community gossip. The pastor reminded me of my responsibilities to God and the church. He reminded me of my talents and my work, and he told me of the need for workers in the vineyard. Talk about the shepherd coming to get a lost sheep! It was a hard pill to swallow then, but I am so grateful for his efforts. Like God and Mom, the pastor did not give up on me. I am sure that prayers were being sent up all around me by family members, however I had completely shut them out. Once again I would learn about life the hard way. I do not know why I continued to take the most challenging roads in life. Often I hear, "No test, No testimony," so I can certainly testify about domestic abuse. In order to be equipped for my journey now, I was being equipped then. From that relationship, my advice is simple: do not fall victim to domestic violence. It did not solve anything, the relationship did not last, and he continued to do what he wanted to do.

In the midst of all of the confusion, I never stopped attending school. I drove to Troy State University every day. I was excited to know that I had only two years left in order to complete my BS degree. I had finally decided to follow in mom's footsteps and become an elementary school teacher.

I have fun memories of Troy, especially with my children. It was always a treat for them to ride to school with me. I remember them going to classes with me and sitting in class coloring. I also recall the number of friends that would watch them while I would attend classes. For the kids, however, the thrill came in going to the student center for a personal pan pizza from Pizza Hut. There was not a local Pizza Hut in Georgiana, so it was always fun for them. I enjoyed watching them enjoy; I would hope that those quality moments in some way influenced them to attend college. Most of all, I hope that my children will always treasure that quality time, and as they rear their children, I want them to remember that quality time beats quantity.

After about two years of the abusive relationship, I finally had enough. He was gone, and I had one year left at Troy. It was Thanksgiving night, and I was angry with Daddy and Tommy, my father's oldest son; thus I decided to go out. I had one friend who did not drink. She naturally became the designated driver, and off we went to the club. While sitting there drinking, I met who would soon become my second husband.

The next few months would go by like a whirlwind. I was traveling back and forth to Anniston, Alabama; my future husband was traveling; I was doing my student teaching, struggling to finish college; and I was back in church stronger than ever. As the time drew near to graduation, it seemed as though everything in school would fall apart. My student teaching experience was great, but I was nicely informed by my math instructor that my writing skills were lacking. She suggested tutoring. My countenance fell sharply. How could they let me get to the end before I was told? To top it all off, I had one instructor that I never could receive any grade above a C in. I was determined to make at least a B before leaving school in her class. I learned that sometimes it just does not matter how you try and what you do; life will deal you an unfair hand. Now I know some battles you just do not worry about fighting.

The following August I graduated from Troy State University, got married, and moved to Anniston, Alabama—all within two days. "I thought I could."

Chapter 6

Having it All

"For what is a man profited, if he shall gain the whole world, and lose his own soul? Or what shall a man give in exchange for his soul?
—Matthew 16:26

My move to Anniston would be the beginning of my professional career, which has been somewhat of a rollercoaster ride and an eye opener to real life. We moved to Anniston on the same day that we married, August 8, 1992. I had dated an older gentleman from Butler County that I met while getting drunk at the local night club in Greenville, Alabama, on Thanksgiving night. We appeared to hit it off immediately. He did not miss a beat coming to Georgiana to see me, and I did not miss a beat going to Anniston. So here I was after a short courtship, married and in Anniston.

The move to Anniston was by far a positive move for the children. We were well provided for, going from our shack to a nice middle-class neighborhood. There we had a three-bedroom, split-level house, a nice fenced-in front yard and back yard, three vehicles, and everything that society deemed necessary to be middle class. As if that was not enough, we were one of the only two minority families in the neighborhood. I was in heaven—or at least, I thought I was.

The children were fine. They both were enrolled in Calhoun County schools and were doing well. When we first arrived, we meet two families that would become very dear to my heart. Together, families flourished and grew together; we were very much like an extended family, and as the children grew up, they found jobs together, rode to school together, and became like brothers and sisters. The adult friendships parted with time and space only. The children remain in touch with each other.

The children participated in all the normal activities. I always told my children that I could not afford to allow them to participate in everything, and thus they were to choose one thing and we would put our effort, time, and money into that. For Tae, it was wrestling; he loved the sport. Talarrius played Pee-Wee football, later became a member of a band, and finally find his niche with wrestling. He was great on the drums and equally as wonderful at wrestling. I enjoyed watching him do both. Talarrius won the state wrestling title early in his tenth-grade year; he would win first place in the years to follow. We spent summers going to wrestling camps and doing the things that would help him improve. My fondest memories are us traveling to camps, getting lost, and having fun. I was the team mom and always got funny looks because most times it would be five or six boys, Quenita, and me traveling; we were the only African Americans with a van full of Caucasian boys that called me Momma. I always had my sons, as I called them.

Quenita was outgoing. She was the class president for many years until she was blackballed. She was also the first African American to be crowned Miss Saks Junior High and Miss Saks High School. Her tenure would last until her junior year in high school, when the band director called me backstage and told me that the judges who had been judging for the past few years felt that someone else should be crown. Thus they discussed it and decided as a panel to lower Quenita's scores to provide someone else with an opportunity to win. Reality set in that I was still black in America. Quenita was also given an opportunity to choose what extracurricular activity she would pursue, and for her it was pageants. Our quality time for two years would be spent on Interstate 20 going to Atlanta for pageants and training sessions. She loved it and it paid off. Although I did not understand how and what being a beauty pageant would do to assist her in life, after meeting her trainer and watching her spend countless hours learning to interview correctly, rephrase questions, and sit like a lady, it finally hit me. The outside beauty, the dresses—none of that mattered. It was the interview skills that she would take with her for the remainder of her life that was important. She never won a state pageant, but in every pageant that she entered, she won the best interview award.

I had accomplished a lot in four years. I now had a stable home complete with a husband and children. I was working in the Talladega School District and was finally a teacher. I worked long and hard at Stemley Road Elementary, I enjoyed my work very much, and I was determined to be a success. In 1994, I returned to school to obtain my master's degree in elementary education. I had the bug—the more education I obtained, the more I wanted. I could not learn enough quickly enough.

The window of opportunity appeared to be wide open. In 1995, I completed my MS in elementary education from the University of Alabama. In the fall of that year, I enrolled at Jacksonville State University to pursue an add-on in educational leadership. I now wanted to be an administrator. In one year I had completed all of the course work in that field. In 1998, I started classes again, this time to earn my educational specialist degree in educational leadership; I completed that degree in 2001.

My mind was set on degrees and climbing up the ladder as quickly as I could, but life would not be as simple as it appeared. Reality soon set in; life in the real world was hard and unfair. In 1997, I had my first reality check about life and its unfairness. I was forced to resign from my position in Talladega County. It was a heartbreaker as well as an eye-opener about the role of politics in education. Everything had appeared be going along smoothly in my life, and all of a sudden it came to a halt. A turn of events would once again send my life in a whirlwind. In one short period, I resigned my position, my father went to prison, my oldest brother died an untimely death, his son died a few months later, and I was forced to take a job paying half the salary that I had been making.

As I look back on that year and everything that happened, even though the bad seemed to outweigh the good, there was some good. One of the things that I cherish most from 1997-98 is Marion Martin. During all of the sadness, I came to meet my best friend while employed in Talladega. In the same year that my life seem to be falling apart, I stumbled upon her. She was a well-rounded lady versed in everything, and she could fit in with any crowd. We hit it off instantly. It seemed as though we had so much in common. It was amazing how a simple conversation about a sapphire ring led to a lifelong friendship. Marion became my best friend. Soon, I was spending time with her family, and they were spending time with us.

Chapter 7
Love Never Fails

Love is patient, love is kind. It does not envy,
it does not boast. It is not rude, it is not self
seeking, it is not resentful. Love does not keep
a score of wrongs. Love stays away from the
negative and it rejoices in truth. Love bears all
things, believes all things, hopes and endures all
things. Love never fails.

—Corinthians 13:4-8)

I had had it all—or I had thought that I did. Soon, I
would find out that I had nothing. I did not have my father,
I did not have my brother, I did not have my nephew,
and there was not enough money in the world to replace
those things. Money for my husband was the answer for
everything, and with that difference of opinion, soon I
understood the scripture that stated the love of money was
the root of all evil. The love of money would cost my dad
forty-two months of freedom. The love of money would
drive a wedge between my husband and me. The love of
money would cause family members and family relationships

to split. On the other hand, I would experience firsthand true love.

We would never miss a visit to Fort Walton, Florida, to see Dad. Mom was determined to go. She was in her early seventies when it all started. I remember the call: Mom simply said, "They have your daddy." I immediately left Anniston and headed for Montgomery to the federal building. There I would find a string of men being lead into a courtroom, all dressed in bright orange jumpers with shackles on their hands and feet. I cannot tell you how my heart dropped to see Daddy; that is a sight that I would not care to see again in my lifetime, and that I hope no one would ever have to see or experience. Daddy simply turned to me and said, "Baby, get my wallet." His voice was so gentle, as if he was saying, "I am sorry."

In Georgiana, I would find that the DEA had gone through everything that my parents owned. My mother was a wreck. People were calling and standing around looking, and I was lost for words. However, my daughterly instinct kicked in. I immediately took Mom to Pensacola to stay with her sister while I tried to sort out what had happened. I did not want her to witness any more than she had to. The media was there; there were phone calls for interviews and question after question. The headline read, "City Councilman Arrested." I had no idea what to say or not to say. Dad had tried to warn me that this was coming, but it just went over my head. Obviously he had a feeling about what might happen. I did not want to hear what he was saying. The federal agents were doing a sweep through Florida and Alabama, and many of Dad's associates had already been arrested. To date, I don't thoroughly understand what happened. Nothing was taken from the house, our other properties, or the bank accounts. Nothing was taken but my daddy. That was enough. He was arrested on drug conspiracy charges.

The next three years would be trying times for our family. We traveled back and forth from Anniston to Georgiana to Fort Walton at least twice a month. We went equipped with quarters in hand. We would be there when the doors opened and stayed as long as we could. The children learned to play dominos and solitaire, and we ate a lot of popcorn. Even in what most people would consider a bad situation, we learned to make lemons out of lemonade. We had great times visiting Dad. The drives and imprisonment forced me to spend time with my parents that I would not have spent otherwise. It allowed my children an opportunity to spend time with their grandparents. Most important, we learned not to judge. There were many men in that prison—educated and uneducated, rich and poor, black and white. We made friends for life. Many times people ask and wonder why my heart is for the underdog or why I can relate to all people, and the answer lies in my life experiences. This experience allowed me to see a lot of things differently.

During this time it became obvious to me that my husband really did not care about me. He never once went to visit my father, offer to drive me to Georgiana, offer to drive me to Fort Walton, or even provide money for gas or food on the journey. His true colors came out.

My mom's colors came out as well,. She hung in there for Dad, although she did not attend the trials; she always said she couldn't take seeing Dad like that. I never missed a trial; I was young and did not have any knowledge about the law, much less what a conspiracy was. We spent all the money we had and could borrow to get Dad a lawyer. I met with the lawyer and discussed the situation. It is amazing how some things you block from your memory. I can't remember the lawyer's name or many of the things we discussed. It all seems like a nightmare that I have awakened from now. The meetings with the lawyers, the trials, the conversations between my brothers and I—these are just a faint memory now. Love stays away from the negative and rejoices in truth. I guess my love for Daddy and my family kept me moving and took away the pain.

The law stated that his incarceration was grounds for divorce. Mom easily could have gotten a divorce and left Dad hanging, but against all odds and what people recommended, she continued the vault business and rented the houses. Before Dad left for prison, he had burglar bars custom made and put on the windows, and he ordered special doors for Mom's safety. Friends fell by the wayside. Many people that once were all around were nowhere to be found for Dad or Mom. Only a few true friends stood by us. In most instances, they were the ones that we never noticed, but they dropped by weekly to see if Mom needed something.

Momma kept the businesses going. My brothers and I ran the night club. We did the best that we could. Dad did not leave things quite like he had found them. After all, we were women and did not know how to fix things up. I found during this time that no one really wanted to help. Daddy lost a lot of his prized possessions. His buildings were worn from time and the lack of upkeep.

Upon Dad's return home, the club was still running, but the music and clients were quite different. Dad could no longer tolerate the music or the young people. The best thing that could have happened was closing the club. With every opening, we were risking Dad's return to prison. Frankly, no one could manage what was truly brought in and out of the club atmosphere; it was a risky business.

Everything may have changed on the outside, but one thing remained the same: Mom's love for Dad. I have never seen love run so deep. She gave meaning to the chapter 13 of Corinthians. What is love? It is patient, kind, longsuffering, gentle, not quick to anger, does no wrong, and is not negative. We are talking about that Agape love now. She exhibited this in every sense of the word. She never missed a beat for Dad. She took the rides, she sat all day, and she ignored people's mumbles and stares. For better or worse, richer or poor, sickness or health, she hung in there. That was unconditional love.

The children and I were able to witness that kind of love. We were there with them every step of the way. Not only that, but my two wonderful children stepped up to the plate for me. They were not legally old enough to drive and not experienced enough, but Talarrius and Quenita would sometimes drive the full-size van back to Anniston on many Sunday mornings after I had worked in the club all night. Sometimes I would feel Tae running off the road in the van and hear Quenita laughing, but I would be so tired that I would just pray that we made it safely home. Love bears all things, believes all things, and hopes and endures all things. Many prayers were answered during this time. God's love kept us safe and together as we traveled.

When it was time for Dad to come home, Quenita trailed me to the halfway house to leave a car for Dad to drive home. It was over. Love had endured.

Chapter 8

Lost and Alone

Save me O God! For the waters have come up
to my neck. I sink in deep mire, Where there is
no standing; I come into deep waters Where the
floods overflow me. I am weary with my crying;
My throat is dry; My eyes fail while I wait for
my God.

—Psalm 69:1-3

Women are lost and alone more often than not. The sad part is that they really don't realize the loneliness. We are mothers, wives, professionals, friends, and lovers, and yet we are still alone. We are like the children of Egypt, wandering around in the wilderness. We are unaware of our priorities, unknowledgeable about directions for our lives. Thus we begin to sink in the deep waters of everyday life. I sank hard.

My life had been surrounded with the daily activities of being a wife and mother. I was determined to give my children what I deemed a normal life. Even though I was in my second marriage, I had read about and, as an educator, valued what society said about children living in a two-parent home. After all, I was a teacher, I was now educated, and I knew what the world deemed as acceptable when it came to a family. Making the transition from being a single, uneducated parent to having an ideal life was just grand! We had the stereotypical family van, and then the SUV, the truck, and the car. We had a three-bedroom home in a middle-class neighborhood, a two-car garage, a big fenced-in yard, flowers beds, and all the things that society considered important. My husband at the time provided a comfortable living environment. I arose early with my husband, woke the children, and prepared breakfast and lunch most days for them, all while preparing myself for work.

I worked hard and long as an educator, determined to succeed and be the very best. Good teachers really do not know when to say when; their days are long and tiring. The days for great teachers seem to never end. Now, I know that they should.

For many years, I picked up and delivered children to their extracurricular activities. I drove to band booster meetings, wrestling meetings, and to Atlanta for weekly pageant training. I prepared dinner and went to class, making sure the kids' homework was done.

Now that I am reflecting back, it is no wonder I was lost and alone. There was no systematic method to doing all that had to be done. It wouldn't be until much later that I realized that God wasn't in the picture, even though the children and I frequented church. Love was nowhere in the picture. And for all of those who say, "What's love got to do with it?" the answer is everything. Everything and everybody was more important than God and me. I thought life was right.

When my son finished high school, I was determined to send him to a small institute that could and would guarantee him success or at least a degree. He had not taken part in many sports because of his eyesight, but as I stated earlier, he had excelled on the drums and in wrestling. His one true love turned out to be wrestling, and his desire was to continue that career. I found a small school in Lebanon, Tennessee, that would meet the criteria of providing a good education and a good wrestling program. Off Tae went to Tennessee—and then the loneliness began.

The ride to drop him off and back would be one that I would never forget. The roads were long and winding, and the mountains took my breath away because I was not familiar with the Tennessee area. I was amazed as we traveled up Interstate 59 to see the mountains and the beautiful land. The drive was much too short; I wanted to savor each moment with my son, because I realized that he would never be my baby boy again. As we drove, it was as though time stood still. I cried all of the way there and all of the way home. For the entire first year that he was gone, when we visited each other, I cried every time he went back to school and every time I would leave him at school.

Life was different at home, but I still had Quenita, and she soaked up the attention of being the only child at home. The activities seemed to double. On top of the activities, I turned my attention to going back to school. Quenita excelled in high school and was attending Jacksonville State as a dual enrollment student. Even though I missed Tae tremendously, Quenita volunteered for enough activities to keep me busy. However, there were still those times that I would sit in Tae's room and long for his return.

Quenita and school became the center of my attention. She was very mature for her age, and with that maturity, I begin to place many day-to-day responsibilities on her. As I would travel back and forth to school, she would take care of many minute details of life for me. I never realized how dependent I was on her until the day she left for Auburn, her school of choice. She was excited about leaving home and attending college, and with great pride the family was eager to see another child enter college.

I thought I was better prepared for her to leave and was up for the task of being alone. Additionally, I was sure that there was no such thing as empty nest syndrome. Boy, was I wrong. The loneliness set in so much more this time than when Tae left. Everything was now gone—at least, that was what I thought.

I believed that now I could turn my attention to my marriage. We had spent little time together in the past years; he was not interested in me at all. He had spent his years building his empire. I thought maybe, just maybe, I could at least tag along during the day while he worked on houses.

That did not happen. Home life was anything but pleasant. My husband could have cared less if I was there or not. As a matter of fact, he once told me, "You do what you want to do, and I am going to do what I want." That was probably the worst thing that he could have told me. That gave me the green light, and I started going out. I was never home. I hated home and being around him. My once perfect life had turned into a disaster.

But as I look back on that time, although he was far from perfect, like so many other ladies I had tossed him to the side for many years. I thought I was doing right. Yes, I cooked, cleaned, folded, and mended, but I forgot to mend *his* brokenness, and I forgot to give him myself. I was busy with the image of a perfect life, but there was no such thing. Life is full of ups and downs, ins and outs. I could not fault him, because he was not the Christian, nor did he ever profess to be the Christian. I thought I was. I handled business with everything but my marriage. There was very little time spent alone together; we simply did not make time for each other.

My favorite time with my husband would be going to a Sunday morning flea market in North Alabama. Those early morning rides were special, but it meant compromising and a day of church. I could not do it often. Another favorite time would be going to a small restaurant in Jacksonville called The Village Inn. These times would be precious stolen moments, moments that every marriage needed on a weekly basis, not just as random acts. These would be two of the only things that we had in common. I realize now that we never stopped to explore the things that we had in common.

He did not go to church, and I loved church. In fact, he once stated that God had not sent him a bill—he did not owe God anything. We were, in every sense of the phrase, unequally yoked. He would often tell me that he could not teach me anything. When I would ask what it was that I was doing wrong in the marriage, he would reply, "If you don't know by now, you will never know." Well I guess I never knew. I had given him what I considered my best at the onset of the marriage. I was in no way perfect, but the verbal abuse in the marriage was unreal.

In my mind, I thought that I was honestly trying to build a home. Yes, the children had taken up much of my life and time. I was at fault in many ways when it came to the children. Like so many women, I was overprotective of my children regarding their stepfather. The fact is if I thought enough of him to marry him, then I should have thought enough of him to make the right decisions in raising my children. If I did not trust his judgment with them, then I should have never married him. I did not allow him to make many decisions as they related to them. I hid many things from him and gave to others even when he said no. Ladies are all too often guilty of that, especially in second marriages. I was at fault because when he married me, the children came with me. In my eyes, he was extremely hard on Talarrius, though he was very gentle and loving to Quenita. It was as if he had a favorite child. His relationship with Quenita would be one of a father and daughter, and I wished I could say the same about Talarrius. That caused me to make up the difference by overly doing on Tae.

Once Quenita left home, I got a job in Roanoke, Alabama, about an hour away from Anniston, which was actually the halfway point between Anniston and Auburn. This would be my first administrative position, and I was so excited. That prior December, I had received my educational specialist degree from Jacksonville State University and had been accepted to and taking classes at the University of Alabama, working toward my doctoral degree. My professional life was flourishing, but my personal life was plummeting. The verbal abuse continued; I never knew what he would say to discredit my character and the things in which I was involved. It was hideous.

On the other hand, life as an administrator was great. I was fortunate enough to get a wonderful principal who was very laid back. I worked hard and spent long hours at work, and many nights I stayed in a local hotel. Maybe that was where I went wrong, but my husband did not seem to care. I put more and more of myself into the job and would find reasons not to go home. I volunteered to serve as the administrator at every extracurricular event.

I knew the owners of the hotel personally, and my room was always available. When I would come home, I would face verbal abuse. I never knew what he was going to say. Once, in front of relatives, he said to me, "I don't know why you are even applying for jobs; you are just a nigger woman. Ain't nobody going to hire you in a high position." I was so embarrassed. As hard as I had worked to attain my administrative certification and specialist degree, he worked just as hard to discredit and discourage me as a professional. After a certain point in the marriage, he stopped supporting my educational process. He told me that I had to use my own money to pay for schooling, and he said that I was stupid to keep going. He did not show up at my last graduation.

Toward the end of 2002, I realized that he really did not care. He made no bones about it. He would tell me that he did not want me. Sex was at a bare minimum; one would think that touching in bed was a cardinal sin. I remember once I placed my foot under his legs, as I often would do, and he kicked my leg off of his with all of his might. When I would attempt to initiate sex, he would blatantly tell me cruel things. "I don't want your stinking pu***; I can get that anywhere." The laundry list of things like this would continue, and it was enough to let me know that he did not want me in bed either.

Little by little, when I would stay at home, I would stay in Tae's room, who had all but stopped coming home. I starting going to the doctor. My nerves were shot, and I was not sleeping. I would jump every time the garage door came up. My body felt as though every nerve inside was crawling. I was sick to my stomach at the thought of being around him. I never knew what to expect or what he was going to say.

By the end of that school term, between giving my all to work and dealing with him, I had all but fallen apart. I was on all sorts of medication. I wanted to leave him and start life over. However, he often told me that no one wanted me. He would remind me of the home we lived in and say things like, "Who else can provide you with what you have here? What little boy are you going to get? What are you going to do, go find yourself a little young punk?" Psychologically he had me, I must admit. After all who would willingly give up the luxuries that I had? How many would sacrifice for the middle-class lifestyle I was living. Even his own brother once told me to just stay, realize what I had, and keep my mouth shut. As I reflect on that, I have to wonder, what is it really like for those women who opt to stay in abusive relationships? How did women of older generations stay with and accept the verbal and physical abuse because of their status, insecurities, and lack of support systems? I can't imagine.

I was taking pills to wake up, pills to go to sleep, and pills to make it through the day. After the 2002-2003 school year ended, I went into a serious state of depression. I can't remember getting out of bed most days. I can't remember driving to work or coming home. What I do remember is that many days I wouldn't go to work. I was writing every day in my journal, praying that God would give me a way out of the situation.

During the spring of 2003, I met a very handsome man who was hurting as much as I was. He, too, was lost and alone, suffering from verbal abuse. Of course there are always two sides to every story, and I only know his side. Thus, in order to disguise his identity, I will speak very vaguely of him. His wife was away all of the time—as a matter of fact, she did not even live with him. We started off as friends, but somewhere along the line we became lovers before ending as friends again. He was someone to talk to; we would take long drives, and there would be so much peace when I was with him. He was tall and handsome, his eyes were beautiful, his voice was soft, his touch was gentle, and his mannerism was chivalrous. He was simple, and life was simple when I was with him. He would make me cherry cola floats and the best coffee I ever had.

I remember as if it was yesterday, he called up and wanted to ride to Chattanooga to eat at Sticky Fingers. We rode all the way to Tennessee just to eat. We would also ride to Tennessee just to see the leaves turning colors in the fall. The pain would disappear for a while, but soon I was dependent on him and on medication.

I wanted more and more of the pleasant solitude that I found when I was with him. I wanted more and more to stay with him and never come home, to be with him against all odds. After all, in my mind, his wife did not want him and my husband did not want me. We spent long hours and many days together, and neither spouse missed or cared about us.

My new position was coordinator of curriculum and instruction for Anniston City Schools. Against everything that my husband had said, I continued to move up the ladder professionally. I was moving quicker than most. This position was one that a far more seasoned person should have received, but God with His perfect plan placed me in it. This position would pay me more than I ever had made. I had great responsibilities and was proud of them. My husband dogged me out, and I was spending more and more time away and with my friend. Life was so bad at home that I would come home and push boxes up against the door to keep him from coming in the room. I would strategically leave work in time to either beat him home or stay at work long enough for him to come home and leave. I had his routine down; once I knew he was gone, I would go home, either eating before I got there or not at all. I knew once I closed up in that room, I was not coming out again until he left. I would go home and do everything that I needed to do before he got back. If I got lucky, something would break at one of his properties and afford me more time.

By November of that year, my husband had gone in the room, read my diary, and read my deepest prayers to God. My prayers were asking for forgiveness of my sins, asking for direction for my life (including life with him), asking God to create in both of us clean hearts, and asking God for deliverance. Sincere and serious prayers of repentance were read by him and eventually would be delivered to his lawyer. I filed for divorce in October 2003 and moved out in November.

Chapter 9

Alone Again—Where Do I Go from Here?

The steps of a good man are ordered by the Lord: and he delighteth in his way. Though he fall, he shall not be utterly cast down; for the Lord upholdeth him with his hand.

—Psalm 37:23-24

I went to my parents' house for Veteran's Day, telling them about the divorce and everything that I had gone through for the past few years. They both knew more than I thought; parents have a sixth sense about their children. Dad had noticed my shaking and nerve condition, but he never voiced it until that family meeting. Mom knew most things because we talked about everything. Dad told me in no uncertain terms not to go back to the house. I left Georgiana and went to Auburn to visit Quenita. I was buying time until things opened up on Tuesday. Once in Anniston on Tuesday, I immediately starting looking for an apartment. I did not have money, I only had prayer. By the end of the day, I was approved for an apartment. I told the apartment manager that I would take the apartment as is and move in within a few days. I had nothing more than the clothes that I had packed for the weekend. I gave up my rights to almost everything in my husband's house. For at least a month, I slept on an air mattress in the living room of the apartment. Quenita was wonderful; she shared things from her apartment in Auburn, and we used her credit to purchase many basic household items. None of that mattered because for the first time in years I was at peace, and sleep came naturally without medication.

The first few months in the apartment were very different for me. I was alone with no cooking, no running home, no rushing to clean, and a freedom that I had not experienced in a while. I had to readjust to being single and to going to the laundry mat. Everything was different. I could come and go as I pleased with no questions asked and with no one to answer to. I enjoyed church and was able to stay as long as I wanted to without feeling guilty. I was able to have time alone with God.

That Christmas was very simple but special. I had very little money but an extreme amount of joy. I had soon discovered the local Rent-A-Center. I rented a bedroom suite and had been granted an opportunity to get my clothes and the dining room suite. For Christmas, we rented a living room suite, although I still utilized the air mattress. My friend and I had traveled to Foley Shopping, and he had graciously helped me purchase some items for Christmas. Quenita brought home one of her friends, and we had a joyous time.

The greatest gift of that particular year was the birth of my first grandson, Kam'ron. I traveled to Tennessee to witness his birth. Of course I was biased, but he was the most beautiful child in the place, and I immediately became attached. Mid-January would land Kam'ron at my house in the middle of the night. Kam'ron was about three weeks old when the call came from Tae. "Mom, we need someone to keep the baby." Kammy would bring lots of joy into my life; he would teach me to love again. Additionally, I learned many things about taking care of a baby that I had not learned on my own because I always had someone around.

With this all going on, I was still alone. Now that I look back, I thank God for Kammy. Taking care of him was the way that I dealt with the pain of being lonely. Once again I would find myself throwing myself into my work and into Kammy, just as I had done with my children. I ran up and down the road to Tennessee more than I cared to remember. I took him to see his parents and brought them to see him. I did not have a life of my own, but I enjoyed every bit of it. There was no time for me; I was tired from work and from caring for a new born. However, Kammy was just a bandage for what was really a deep-rooted problem. He was a method of transitioning me from one point in life to the next. It is funny how God will make the transitional process easy, but He will also send people, things, jobs, or projects to assist in the process.

Transitioning was my way to shut the outside world away. No one was allowed in my circle. I In my mind, I was beating myself up and having a pity party. What was wrong with me? Why couldn't I keep a husband? What was I doing wrong? Why couldn't I attract a single man? Who would want a woman that had been married and divorced twice? How would I explain it to people? I never thought at that time that I did not owe anyone an explanation. It would be much later in this journey that I realized that I only answered to God.

I was not where God wanted me yet. I was just beginning to walk into the fire to be made over again. As right as it all seemed then, it was all wrong, yet it was working together for my good. That was a time for cleansing, for renewal. It was a time to start stripping me. God had to strip away the layers of depression, low self-esteem, self-pity, guilt, and loneliness.

I stayed in the apartment for six months, and in May 2005, I rented a beautiful home on the east side of Anniston in an older, quiet neighborhood. Talarrius had moved to Anniston and was now in the apartment in which I had previously resided. My new house sat on top of a hill overlooking the city. It was a beautiful scene. The house was older and had been recently had a face-lift, however most of the original structure was still intact. It had three-bedrooms and two and half baths. It had beautiful hardwood floors, a formal living and dining room, a grand room, an attic with a fan, white columns outside, a detached two-car garage, and a beautiful yard. Everything seemed to be falling in place. I had the perfect job while I was raising a grandson, completing my doctoral degree, and making things happen on my own. But that was the problem: I was making things happen on my own—I was not listening to God. Or rather, I was not trying to hear God; I was just doing my own thing. Once again, I was so busy with my life, just as I had been when I was married, that I did not have time for God.

Life for me was a revolving cycle. Every time life would start to improve, I would move God out of the way. I was picking God up and putting Him back down, treating Him like a faucet by turning Him off and on. When life was good, I did not need Him, and when it was bad, I needed Him desperately. Life was so good during this time that I purchased my first home one year later. It was bigger and better—or so I thought.

The year that followed after purchasing the house was very tough. The house was a lemon, though I tried to make lemonade out of it. On the surface it was beautiful, but everything that could go wrong went wrong after the first year. The second year in the house I found myself pumping more and more money into it—money that I did not have. I was taking my mortgage money to pay for repair after repair. Then my car broke down, so I bought a new one. Money was coming in one hand and going out the other.

I was going to church, praying and paying my tithes randomly. I was in regular attendance at church, but prayers were like the faucet, only on when needed.

In April 2005, I felt that all hell had began to break loose. Now I know that I was just continuing my walk through the fire. My perfect job was no more; the superintendent had decided to make major cutbacks, which included my position. I started working for the Georgia State Department of Education. I was excited going in, and I traveled the state for six months, but I lost everything that I had. It took everything that I made and more to travel. Reimbursement for travel was sporadic at best, and even though I was making more money, it took every bit of it to maintain and meet the demands of the job.

In addition to the cost of the job, my boss had made some very prejudice statements that left me uneasy about working in the environment. It was obvious that he was not fond of minorities and that equality did not exist in his world. By November of 2006, I was looking everywhere for a job. I took a job with the Bartow County Schools as an assistant principal, and along with the job came a twenty-thousand-dollar pay decrease. I was devastated. By

June 2007, everything was gone. I had been broken all the way down: my health was gone, my back was hurting, and pain shot down the right side of my body like nothing I had ever felt before. I could not pay any of my bills because my annual salary had decreased, and I was not able to work. For many months I barely made a thousand dollars, a sharp decrease from the five thousand that I was bringing home only six months earlier. Everything was gone.

Chapter 10

Out of the Miry Clay—The Road to Recovery

I waited patiently for the Lord; And He inclined to me, And heard my cry. He also brought me up out of a horrible pit, Out of the miry clay, And set my feet upon a rock, And established by steps. He has put a new song in my mouth—Praise to our God; Many will see it and fear, And will trust in the Lord.

—Psalm 40:2

It was a winter day that was chilly in many ways. One of my two remaining aunts had passed, my mother had taken a fall, and I dreaded meeting the sadness that would be on my father's face as he prepared to bury Aunt Jean. I was traveling down Highway 21 in Lowndes County, Alabama, in the direction provided to me by the men from the local food mart. I was lost, yet I was determined to make it to Camden, Alabama, to see an old friend. We had agreed that it would be a central location for both. It had been years, yet it seemed as though it was yesterday that we were working together at McDonald's. We quickly regained our close friendship. He only had a few hours, and it was imperative that I made it to Georgiana in a timely manner.

As traveled down the lonely highway, I noticed death. There was nothing that resembled life; the highway was long and cold, the houses were old and worn, and the trees were tall and dead. Moss hung from the trees, which were anchored in muddy, miry water. The water level appeared to be extremely high, above flood level; it was very visible and somewhat frightening. I found myself telling God that I was sorry that I had even thought about asking Him to move me to that area. The more I saw of Highway 21, the more I dreaded asking to move, and just the thought of living in such a despairing area . . . The final straw to this drive was the fact that I did not have phone service.

There were many thoughts that crossed my mind as I traveled along this road, which seemed like it would never end. What if something happened to me? No one would ever find me. What if the car broke down? The more I thought, the faster I drove. All I wanted to do was to get off that highway and get to what I considered civilization. I had attempted several times to use the phone, but to no avail. There were no other travelers on the road; it was only me.

Out of nowhere I saw in my rearview mirror a huge, black truck on my tail. I immediately started thinking that this guy was crazy. Why was he following me so closely? My mind starting running a hundred miles per minute with concern. Then the truck pulled over to the side of the car. Again I began to wonder what was wrong. Maybe it was something wrong with my car, and he was trying to warn me? I just could not figure out what was going on.

Finally, the window of the truck came down, and I saw my friend directing me to pull over. Immediately I pulled over and stopped the car. I watched as his door opened, and he stepped out looking more handsome than ever to me. He was like an angel sent to me. He wore a black suede cowboy hat, a black leather jacket, and a black leather cowboy boots, all matching that beautiful black truck. He had a smile that would melt the hearts of most, and I knew at that moment that everything, and I do mean everything would be alright. With his soft-spoken voice he said, "Didn't you see me behind you? I was trying to get your attention so that you would pull over."

"Where did you come from?" I asked.

"I passed you and turned around."

"How did you find me?"

"I knew you were on the wrong highway, I didn't have a signal on the phone, and I knew I had to find you, so I just got on the highway and started driving. I was determined to drive until I found you. Get back in your car and follow me."

It would be weeks after that incident when God revealed and opened my eyes to that experience in an entirely new light. That is what I want to share with you. God is so awesome by using such a personal experience to show me how He cares for His people every day. I learned a lot from that experience, such as my friend had a carrying spirit and that he had my best interest at heart. But as I begin to reflect back on that day and I often do, I see God's hand in it all. I look at that experience through a spiritual eye. God used that experience to illustrate just how far He will go to redeem His children.

The very first thing lesson learned from this experience was a personal eye opener. I realized that life for many of us is like that long, lonesome highway, and at that point in my life, I was on that road. Life for me was not going anywhere; I was stuck in the mud. Everything around me appeared to be dead and cold. My body and spirit were like the houses frayed by the trails and tribulations of life. My self-esteem was stripped like the trees. I was drowning in burdens from everyday life, drowning in debt, and drowning in self-pity, and I did not see a way out of the mire.

Many of you are traveling down a road of despair where nothing appears to be alive. Everything and everyone is negative, and none of your choices appear to be good. Your life is just as I have described that road. But God, just as my friend, came looking for me, and He will come looking for you. It is not God's desire that any of us are lost and left on the lonely highway of life.

For various reasons many people take wrong turns in life, and many are given wrong directions. Some forget the directions or refuse to follow them. When this happens, they find themselves on the lost highway, along with despair and heartache. They find financial difficulties and professional ruin, their spirits battered and broken. They perceive life to be dark and dreary.

God reveals that He will never leave of forsake his children. Like Larry, He realizes when we are on the wrong road and off course. He knows when we are hardheaded and stubborn. He can tell when we fail to follow his directions, and He will come searching for His children.

God knows when our signal is weak and even when we don't have a signal; He can still find us. Oftentimes Christians become so worn by the trials of life, so busy with everyday responsibilities, so busy with careers, so busy with household chores, so busy with children and spouses—and they forget to pray. Realistically, everyone has at some time experienced this phase of forgetting to pray daily. At some point in this Christian journey, sin blocks and weakens the signal. But we serve a God that sits in the highest tower, and no matter where we are and how weak our signal may be, God can still find us. That is praiseworthy.

God revealed that just as my friend was doing everything behind me to get my attention to pull over, I was ignoring him and wondering what was going on. In our walk with God, he does things to get our attention, and we ignore Him. That revelation was painful. As we look back on our lives, we can see subtle hints that God has shown us about many things. If we pray and seek God's advice, He will direct our paths. He provides signs of good and bad, right and wrong all around us. God has placed something on the inside, an alarm that will let us know when something is not right. Some call it a gut feeling and some call it intuition, but whatever we call it, it's God. He does things to get our attention and to direct our path. But all too often we question what is obvious. We ignore the obvious, especially if the obvious is not what we want as a person. How many times has God shown you the right way, given you an answer, provided you with evidence that contradicted your thoughts and feelings—and you simply kept driving? After allowing you to go so far, God will pull up beside you and say, "Pull over; you are going the wrong way," or "Pull over; it is time for me to take the lead." Of course, you have that option to keep driving or to allow God to lead you to safety. I pulled over.

God revealed that He can lead us to safety if we are willing to follow Him. But we must be submissive to Him and to his will. I was on the right highway, but I didn't have a clue about where I was, how far I had to go, or what to do when I got to my destination. As Christians, we are on the right highway, we go to church, we pay our tithes, we go to Sunday school and to mission, and we do all the things we think we are supposed to do—but we really do not have a clue about where we are in life, how far we have to go, or what to do when we get there. God is telling us to stop, pull over, and allow Him to lead the way. The steps of a good man are already ordered by the Lord, so why are we trying to go off-road when a path has already been laid out before us? Allow God to lead your life. I can't explain the joy, the calmness, the peace, and the assurance that I had on that cold winter day, when I drove behind that truck and allowed my friend (and God) to lead me to safety. I cannot explain the feeling I have now, knowing that I have pulled over in my life and am allowing God to lead. There is a calmness, a peace, a joy, and an assurance that everything is going to be all right. I understand that everything still won't go my way, that trials will still come, that the devil is still alive, but I have a peace in knowing who is leading the way.

Chapter 11

Following Him

Then Jesus said to His disciples, "If anyone
desires to come after Me, let him deny himself,
and take up his cross and follow Me. For
whoever desires to save his life will lose it, but
whoever loses his life for My sake will find it.
For what profit is it to a man if he gains the
whole world, and loses his own soul? Or what
will a man give in exchange for his soul? For the
Son of Man will come in the glory of His Father
with His angels, and then He will reward each
according to his works.
—Matthew 16:24-27

I have found God to be so awesome in revealing things
to me at the point in my life. For whatever purpose, He
has used a person to drive home a picture of following
Him. I called Marion with the fantastic plan about leaving
my current residence. I knew if anyone could make me
look logically at both sides of the big picture, she would.
She had always been so good at playing the role of devil's

advocate. I did what I always do: I called her with my plan. I proceeded to tell her that I thought I had accomplished what God intended for me in Anniston and that life was at an all-time low for me in the area. After all, I didn't have family in Anniston; professional associates and church affiliates were basically it. Nothing sustaining that would prevent me from wanting to leave. I was driving 160 miles daily to work and desperately wanted to get back into the Alabama Public School System. I began sending resumes to the various school districts nearest to where I hoped God would ultimately send me.

I walked through my gift from God, my house, and I begin to look at the things that I had acquired throughout my adult years, my marriages and relationships. I thought about the things that were dear to me and why. As I traveled through my living room, I noticed my curio cabinet, which was filled with beautiful redbird crystal from Germany and my first marriage. Oh, how I admired and adored that crystal; I dared not let anyone to touch it. Then I traveled through my dining room. I noticed the beautiful chinaware that was also purchased in Germany. I saw a beautifully decorated dining room table with blue wine goblets, to match the soft blue china. I noticed the beautiful silver chandelier that adorned the center of the table. I noted the fine wine set on the buffet table.

Next, I walked through my kitchen and saw cabinets filled with beautifully decorated brandy glasses, wine glasses, blue cookware, grapevines, and notes across the refrigerator that reflected a past relationship. As I walked down the stairs and into the den, I noticed my butterscotch loveseat and sofa, my television and DVD player, and a room filled with pictures of events that I had attended or hosted. On the wall hung a picture of a replica of a church and people praising the Lord and shouting; it had been given to me at Christmas in 2005. I traveled to my piano room, which was rather empty except for a piano with two broken legs that had traveled with me through three moves. (The guys from the local football team had dropped in twice.) Finally, I went upstairs to my bedroom, and oh, the memories that it housed: stuffed animals, pictures, the bedroom suite, the comforter, the TV, even the clothes in the closet.

You might be asking why is it relevant for me to describe my house. Well, while I was walking through the house, I began to think about how much baggage from past relationships was present all around me. I thought about how each room carried a different message of pain and heartache. I realized each room represented something and someone that I no longer was, and most of all I realized that each time I walked into a room, I was unconsciously reliving each of those relationships and hanging on to the past—the good, bad, and the ugly. Yes, I learned something from each relationship, and everything was not bad, but they were over. It dawned on me that if I was ever going to move forward, I had to let go of the past, even if it meant leaving everything behind. Philippians 3:13-14 reads, "Brethens, I count not myself to have apprehended: but this one thing I do, forgetting those things which are behind and reaching forth unto those things which are before. I press toward the mark for the prize of the high calling of God in Christ Jesus." I wasn't forgetting anything that was behind me, but rather living in the past day after day.

At that moment, I starting calling those near and dear to me. I called my daughter and son and asked them what she wanted from the house. They thought I was crazy. I finally called Marion and told her that she could have not only the living room suite that she had asked for from the beginning, but everything else in the house that she wanted. This may even sound strange to you, but I trusted God for a bright and glorious future, and I knew at that moment in order for me to move in God's glory and in His will, I had to let go of those things that kept me in the bondage of past relationships. If God was going to bless me with a husband, I had to be ready when he came. I knew at that moment that I had to step out on faith and believe that "God would supply all my needs according to his riches in glory by Christ Jesus" (Philippians 4:19). I knew at that moment that I had to deny myself if I was going to follow God's lead.

I thought about denying the self, the disciples and what Jesus asked of them. He asked them to do the exact same thing: give it all up. You are probably saying that it is easier to say than to do. Well, it is a faith issue. As I gave everything away, I didn't have a clue about replacement; I surely couldn't afford anything new. But isn't that like God? Earlier in Philippians 4, you will find my theme: "I can do all things through Christ who strengthens me." I know beyond a shadow of a doubt that God will do what he has promised. The disciples didn't suffer, so why should I? He is the same God today as He was then. Our problem today is that we don't trust Him to be faithful to His word. We don't believe God to keep His promises. We don't walk out on faith. I read a sign on a church bulletin that said, "Put Your Faith to Work."

There are many of you today, holding onto baggage and refusing to deny yourself of many things for various reasons. Denying yourself can take place in many forms. Denying myself meant the things I held to be valuable in my home, things that I fought to keep in each relationship, things that I thought made my home unique and made me, things that provided me with a conversation when others would walk through the house. But in order for me to follow God's lead in a new relationship with Him, I needed to give up all of those things. As I entered into the intimate relationship with God, I didn't need to bring the beds and gifts of adulterous relationships with me. I didn't need to bring the glasses of drunkenness with me, I didn't need to bring the pictures of parties with me, I didn't need to bring the spirit of depression with me, and I didn't need to bring the arguments and disappointments with me. No, I needed to come just as I was: weary, worn, sad, and trusting God for deliverance. I needed to deny myself of everything that kept me separated from God.

What things are you holding on to? What things are keeping you from following Jesus, and how do you determine what those things are?

The first step in denying the self is to step back and evaluate yourself realistically. Take a look inside and out. That is hard to do; many of us do not want to really take a look at the sins that we have committed and still commit. It is easier to look at everyone else's problems. It is easier to make excuses for what we are doing wrong. It is easier to justify why we are doing wrong rather than to confess. That is not a true examination of self. Truth hurts, often deep within. Once we examine ourselves, we will find a lot of pride and vanity. There are so many things in this everyday life that is simply not necessary. We throw away far more than we save. We evaluate things in life that are not important. We are caught up in man's idea of right and wrong versus God's.

Once you have taken that look inside and out, you will find many areas that truly need to be denied. I found that I was holding onto baggage for conversational pieces,

I bought items and wore certain clothing, I went to the beauty salon, and I even ate certain items for the purpose of creating conversation. Yes, ladies, we all do it, and that is just a fact. In some form or fashion, as we search ourselves, we will see many areas that we need to deny ourselves of. When we deny ourselves of conversational items, then there is room for God.

PART III
I Will

Chapter 12

His Plan for My Life

For I know the thoughts that I think toward you,
saith the Lord, thoughts of peace, and not of
evil, to give you an expected end. Then shall ye
call upon me, and ye shall go and pray unto me,
and I will hearken unto you. And ye shall seek
me, and find me, when ye shall search for me
with all your heart.

—Jeremiah 29:11-13

I felt broken by my life in Anniston. The potter saw a
vessel that was broken by the winds of life, and He sought
with so much compassion to make me over again. Yes, I
was the vessel that no one thought was good. I cried, "Lord,
you are the potter, and I am the clay; make me over again
today." That day, God picked up the pieces of my broken
heart and began to make me over. Now that I had taken the
walk through the house and found all the aches and pains, I
had given everything away but just a few items. The doctors
had worked fiercely in Anniston to find the source of my
agonizing pain, but to no avail. Mother's condition was not

improving. I could not pay my bills because my pain had not allowed me to work a complete pay period in months. Everything that had been given was suddenly taken away. Thus I realized that it was finally time for me to take up my cross and follow him. It was time for me to stop fighting the directions given and give in and let God take control. It was time for me to close that chapter in my life.

My new beginning would land me in Montgomery, Alabama. At that time I did not understand why, however as I complete this book, I know that "I will" would be the reason for the location. I did not want to return to Georgiana. I had heard the saying "There is nowhere like home," but for me Georgiana would no longer be home. The people I knew, the places I had gone, and the things I would do were no longer there. More important, I went to my own, and they did not receive me. Church for me was cold. I had heard so many times that one gets out of service what one puts into it. I had every intention of going home to my home church and working as hard as I had in other churches.

I started searching for a job in March 2007; even in pain, I knew that I must leave Anniston. Georgia had not been a good move, but I realize now that it was the method that God had used to force me out of a city. I had known for a while that my season was up in Anniston, but I refused to listen to the voice of God. The final year in Anniston would be the worst by far. I was living in Anniston and was working based out of the heart of Atlanta in the Twin Towers, as some called them. I remember the first day that I arrived in Atlanta to work; I was like a kid in a candy store. The city was big and exciting, and the building was tall and beautiful. I was excited about riding the MARTA and experiencing the sounds sights that the city had to offer. It would not take long for me to discover the Underground. Better yet, it did not take long for me to realize that it took all of five minutes to walk to the underground from my small little cubical on the seventeenth floor. I immediately fell in love with walking next door and watching people from all walks of life enjoy the local attractions. The breeze on the outside of the building was very refreshing and always allowed for a little talk with God. It also served as a calming force when all seemed to go wrong at work.

I had driven across the state of Georgia working for the Department of Education and had witnessed racism like never before. Georgia was worse than Alabama. There were cities that I was afraid to go to as a minority and cities that I was warned about before I would leave my office. But the greatest shock was the racism that I experienced firsthand at the Department of Education. It was shocking to hear a department head comparing an African American to Buckwheat in a social setting without hesitation. At that point, I knew that I was in the wrong place. If the traveling had not broken me down physically, working under leadership that referred to African Americans in that manner had broken my desire to work for the organization. I was disappointed and my spirit was broken. Like many others, I was sure that once I went to Georgia to live, life would be grand. However, it quickly became apparent that this was not my appointed place.

After six months at the State Department of Education, and in debt more than ever from travel and a slow reimbursement, it was time from me to find something new.

A friend who had attended the University of Alabama with me had also left the DOE and taken a position with the Bartow County School System in Cartersville, Georgia.

My total dissatisfaction with my current position caused me to start the search for a job again. For me, the greatest struggle would be the salary. My salary need was greater than ever. I remember praying and asking God to lead me; I did not want my salary to decrease. It was during this time that God would reveal His plan for my life.

It had been years since I remembered a dream, but this was like no other dream. I saw myself on a website. The website evolved in my dream, right down to the details of what pictures to place on it. During that dream-vision, God spoke and gave me clear directions. I woke the next morning and said, "Lord, I will." Just to tell you how God works, the picture that I saw on the website had been taken months earlier, and I did not purchase them. I got up early the next morning, hurried to the photographers, and begged him to find the pictures I had taken earlier in the summer. After searching, they found the photos stored on a disk. How many photographers do you know keep pictures not purchased on a disc? I purchased the pictures and set out to find someone to build a website. It would not take but an afternoon to discover that one of my former teachers could and would build the webpage and all of the particulars that went with it. It was not fancy, but it was what I could afford at the time, and after all, it was God's design. So it was that "IKAN Ministry—Empowering Women, Changing the World" was born.

Driving across the state for the next few days would be wonderful—time well spent with God. He spoke consistently in my spirit, giving me topics for the webpage; He gave me messages and directions faster than I could move. God's was pouring things into my spirit like water freely falling from a fall, and it was wonderful. Soon I was sending weekly devotionals to women, and soon those women were sending thank-you notes to me.

The excitement would last as I found myself on a new job in Bartow County, Georgia. There I was an assistant principal at a middle school. God had moved me, and along with the move came a huge salary decrease, but what could I say? I asked for a move. Now I realize that the move and location would serve a greater purpose: it would give me stability. Yes, the salary was quite a bit less, gas was really expensive, and I struggled with money. However, now as I look at it, God was simply keeping me employed. Even though I had said, "Yes, Lord, I will do whatever you want," I was still saying no with my heart.

Things started to fall apart. As Murphy's Law stated, everything that could go wrong went wrong. Everything was breaking down at the house. I had water leaks everywhere and could not find anyone to fix them. Every time I thought I had found someone, something would come up. I was so determined to fix constant leaks in one of my bathrooms, and I went in one night with my pliers, took off the fixtures in the bathtub, and succeeded in making a mess. I forgot one simple step: I forgot to turn off the water. I did not know what to do. I could not plug the hole up. I remember that my ex-husband would turn the water off outside if there was not a shut-off valve inside, so outside I went with the pliers. I could not get the water off. I called everyone I knew, to no avail. Finally, I reached an associate who had worked with Anniston City Schools, and soon he was on his way. In the meantime, while waiting for him to call back, I had called the City Water Board, and they responded. I cannot tell you how embarrassed I was. Thirty-five dollars would be the cost added to my water bill for that after hours call. The water was turned off from the outside, and my co-worker and I were able to repair the bathtub on the next day. The next few weeks would bring leaks from the outside, problems with my car, problems in my relationship, sickness with Mom, and unbearable pain in my back and leg. The life I had known for the past three years was quickly going downhill. Signs from God were everywhere, but I had not kept my end of the bargain. I refused to leave Anniston and was hanging on only by a thread. Every day brought more emotional and physical pain. Depression was setting in quickly. I had been down that road so many times before. I would stay home from work for days, sometimes even a week. My paycheck was quickly becoming less and less, but I did not care. Life as I knew it was gone, and I just wanted to stay home. I did not have the money to make ends meet, and I was sick and hurting. I tried to work, giving it my best shoot. I enjoyed my job, but by the end of school, I was physically, emotionally, and spiritually drained.

By the end of May 2007, I had resumes posted on websites across Alabama. I just wanted to move home at this point. My goal was to get closer to my parents. The doctors still did not give me clear-cut answer about Mom's health. I had gone home several times to find her consistently losing weight. Her once size-fourteen body was now frail and down to a size eight. Everything was falling off of her, and no one had an answer. That worried me. I spent a lot of time in Georgiana. I interviewed as close as I could to home. I spent a lot of time with my parents, and a lot of time repenting. This time alone with them, away from my life, afforded me an opportunity to see the things at which I had failed as a daughter. Once again, I found myself asking God to forgive my shortcomings toward my parents and Him. The errors of my ways and my selfishness had become obvious. My quest for success had overpowered what was truly important in life, God and family. I was so embarrassed by myself, but somehow God still looked beyond my faults and saw my needs. I once again had to tell Him, "Lord, I will do you will, whatever it is that you would have me to do." I had a new outlook on life, and I was determined to get closer to Mom and Dad.

The job hunt was on. It seemed as though I had applications everywhere, but no one was calling. May soon ended, and I was over qualified, or no one wanted to match my salary, or nothing was open at the time. I had never been in a situation quite like this. I was beginning to worry. In the course of the past seven years, I had always worked during the summer, and here summer was quickly approaching, but I did not have a job. I was not going back to Georgia.

A friend told me to use my resources to find me a job. He told me to call in favors. In his words, "Surely from all your years of recruiting, you know someone that knows of your skills and reputation that will give you a job." I had always been independent, and I did not want to use anyone. I had spent three years in Anniston helping people get jobs in the system, and I had spent countless hours helping others fill out applications for jobs and teacher certificates. I had spent countless hours telling others how the Teacher Certification Office for the State Department of Education worked, and I convinced them to return to school to be teachers—and here I was without a job and no interviews. After all, in every school system that I had worked in, I was able to convince someone to go back to school and either get an education or further their education. I was known for encouraging others, but little did they know that I needed encouraging as much as anyone else.

Finally I called an old recruiting friend and ended up in Bullock County, Alabama, for a job interview. As I was traveling down Interstate 85, I glanced to the left, and there set a beautifully landscaped apartment complex. At that moment God softly spoke in my spirit, and I knew at that moment that the complex was going to be my new place of residence. After four hours of chatting with the superintendent in Bullock County, I stopped at the apartment office. I did not have credit; it was totally shot from trying to make ends meet on half a check along with everything else. But I graciously went inside, explained my situation, and completed an application. Of course they told me I needed to put down a hefty deposit, but I toured the grounds and fell in love with it. It was so peaceful and beautifully landscaped, with a man-made lake in the center with ducks. The staff was wonderful, and I was in love with the Verandas at Mytlene. I immediately called my parents, and within two weeks, I was in Montgomery.

I came to Montgomery with God, a car, bedroom furniture, a pieced-up living room, my great-grandmother's hundred-year-old dining room set, clothes, dishes, a few appliances, and some junk. Everything else was gone. I had placed the house on the market, hoping it would sell before they foreclosed on it, but it did not. Another strike. But I was here. I had taken up my cross and followed His directions. How did I know? It's simple: everything just fell in line, right down to the money. It took everything I had and a loan from Dad, but I made it.

Along with the above items, I brought with me severe physical and mental pain. I had a prescription for physical therapy, as well as no job and no prospect of getting one. The entire month of June would be a time of only God, me, and physical therapy. The physical therapy was not helping;

I was in pain daily, I barely could walk, and I knew that I was not physically able to work. Day in and day out I was in the bed gaining weight. I got up only to go to church, check mail, and get fresh air.

Finally, at the end of my therapy session, my physical trainer recommended that I go to see a specialist in Montgomery. After he reviewed my records, he could not believe that no one had conducted a nerve study. Well, I had gone to a neurologist at Princeton in Birmingham, who only told me to do what the doctor in Anniston told me to do. At that point, I was totally devastated and ready to throw in the towel. I agreed to the PT's advice, realizing that I needed to get all the help that I could, because I could see the possibility of working in pain, though still there were no calls for interviews. I also knew that I would only have limited insurance coverage if I did not receive a job. After two brief tests, the neurologist was able to tell me that the nerves on the right side of my body had been damaged. Finally, someone could give me an answer. I thought I was going crazy; maybe the pain really was not really there. God had to move me from Anniston to Montgomery in order for me to be diagnosed. That was a start, and even as I sit today writing, I am not healed; I am in pain, and there is still the possibility of surgery, but I at least know what is wrong and that someone is working on it. But if I had not taken up my cross and followed His lead, I would not be where I am now.

It was certainly a trust issue. I had to trust God to lead me; I had to take up my cross and follow Him, just not walk around the house after He had spoken to me, avoiding what He told me to do. It is hard sometimes to follow God, especially when we do not know where we are going and what will happen when we get there. Following

Jesus is commitment; it demands a choice—sometimes a hard choice—that we may not fully understand. Like the disciples, if I was to be totally committed to Him, I would have to deny my desires and follow His lead.

I made God a promise, after spending much needed time with my parents, that I would do what He told me to do, that I go where He told me to go, and that I would say what He told me to say. That was a promise that I would keep against all odds. Talking about a relationship with God, but not trusting him and following his lead, is meaningless. I finally realized that. God had to bring me to a complete place of peace, rest, and dependence on Him—all to make me hear His voice. He had given me directions months earlier through a vision of what I was to do, and I failed. I was worrying about what friends, family, Mom, Dad, and my children would say. But it would be this experience that would really drive home the point that if I was to be blessed, I had to deny myself, take up my cross, and follow Him. It is much easier to volunteer for God's army and volunteer to be under his authority than it was for Him to force you to a place as He has done me. I had just been a rebel. Thank God that He continued to look beyond my faults and see my needs.

This for me would not be easy. God had a plan for my life, one that He had shared will me, and in order for me to walk in my appointment, I would be like the disciples, but also like Ruth: my commitment to God would force me to leave my family and homeland. Not in the physical sense, but the spiritual realm. This calling would force me to go against all that I had been taught and ever believed to be true. How would I ever tell Mom that her daughter, who had been brought up in a Baptist Church and did not believe or accept women ministers, had been called into the ministry?

That was the million-dollar question. Everyone else in the family would receive the news and rejoice with me—but not Mom and not all members of my home church. I knew that from the start, but frankly that was just life.

God had blessed me by this time in so many ways. He had provided me with a job five days before school would start—against all odds, against what everyone thought. He had blessed me to once again have a job in administration. Everyone had prepped me and told me that I would not receive a job in administration. They said, "Katrina, you will probably just have to go back in the classroom and start over. It is hard to get into another system and start at the top. Just be satisfied with what you can get." But God said, "Ask whatever you will in My name. I would give you the desires of your heart. All power is in My hand." I asked and I received. I was the new assistant principal at McIntyre Middle School. God had an appointed place for me, and I had to wait until the appointed time and place to receive the blessing—and a blessing it turned out to be.

McIntyre Middle School was equipped with three powerful ministers and a strong God-fearing principal. God sent me there and it would be there that I would find my spiritual father and spiritual brother. For the first time, I would find someone that I could relate to and have a conversation with; not competition, just brothers in Christ. It was a joy to work with and be around. Furthermore, I would find a Christian boss who made coming to work a pleasure even on bad days, because he was understanding. Even in pain I enjoyed my job, and for the first time in years, I did not mind getting up and going to work. The funny thing was that my salary was lower than it had been in five years, and although I worked afterschool programs and on Saturdays, I still did not mind. I could not explain it, but the salary did not matter; nothing could beat the peace of mind that I now had. It was God putting back the pieces of my life, one small bit at a time.

But then all of a sudden, things started happening in lightning speed. Before I knew anything, I had found a church home, New Pleasant Valley AME Zion Church. Yes, I would change from my Baptist roots to Methodist. I found peace and God's spirit within the four wall of this small church in Hope Hull, Alabama, a church that was bursting at the seams. So many people were hungry for the word, and there was so much work to be done—so many ministries to be organized, so many hurting women. It would be here that God would place me for a season away from my home church.

Although I was happy to have found a church home, I was deeply saddened that I had gone to my home family and was not received. It was my desire to give my all to my home church, but I learned through this experience that we could plan and God could unplan, and that's all I will say about that.

I had a job and a church home, and then out of the blue the pastor came to me and said, "Katrina, it's time to set up your initial sermon and get you licensed." That sent me for a loop and into deep prayer. I was really toiling with this, because even then I was fighting the call. But again, God just spoke in my spirits as I slept one Sunday after church, and I knew all was well. It looked as though my life was complete. God was really working, but He wasn't finished yet.

October 18, 2007, I would marry Marvin Lavon Smith. I married my best friend (of course next to Marion) of approximately thirteen years. We had been friends for about sixteen years, and I knew he was my best friend even though I was not always his best friend. On the day of our marriage, however, it was our fairytale come true.

I meet Marvin in the early 1990s. He was the DJ at the club that my family ran. We were business partners, we were friends, we were lovers, and we had committed adultery. Our union would not be a typical one; I can only say that it was God's divine purpose and plan, and we would work together for God now like we had worked together for Satan then. We met at the club and during a time under his surge name, La-La Fresh. He was just that, but there was always some underlying factor that I was able the see that went beyond the DJ persona. He was sweet and gentle, mild and kind. He was energetic and enthusiastic. His heart was huge, his laughter robust, his patience long, and his determination unbelievable.

We helped each other. His name drew a crowd for the club, and my relationship with God and my writing abilities drew a crowd for him in church. He was always called on to speak. We were a team and unstoppable team throughout the nineties. We were young and foolish; we made money and threw it away.

Marvin always told me that one day he would marry me. He had said that we were meant to be together, but I never trusted or believed him. Why would I want a DJ that everybody wanted? I only wanted him for a season, and that season was when I needed a friend. He never failed to be there, but I failed so many times for him. I would only answer his calls when the relationship that I was in was shaky. I never thought that he might need my friendship. For at least six years, he was really on my list. He moved to Cleveland, Ohio with his friend, who played for the NBA, so I thought that got him out of my life. I would at best sporadically answer his calls, but Marvin never stopped calling. Then they moved to Indiana, and he still called. The harder I fought to stay away, the harder he pushed to stay. After all, I was in control, and when I would not answer, he would simply leave me a message and end it with, "I Love You." He never gave up on me, and this reminds me so much of how God never gives up on us; He simply leaves us a message: "I Love You."

Marvin came to visit in July. I was reluctant about his coming. My wall of protection was still very high, and I was still pushing him away. We had mentioned marriage before casually, but this time he was different—he was ready, and I could see it all over him. I, on the other hand, was not. He asked me to marry him, and I said yes, though I was still relatively unsure. After all, he had not married and settled down yet, and he was forty years old.

I knew that I needed someone in my life, and I had asked him to come and take care of me. I trusted him. We were best friends, and there were no secrets between us. So what was the problem? I could not see the forest for the trees. I had been praying about the marriage quite a bit, and one day while walking around the lake, God spoke and reminded me of what I had asked for: God reminded me of all the things that I done to Marvin, and how Marvin continued to love me in spite of it. God reminded me that this man had waited sixteen years and loved me, even when I did not love myself. He reminded me that I had not put specifications on my request, I had just asked Him to send me a husband that would love me unconditionally. At that point, I let my guard down and asked for forgiveness, and I felt a renewing of the mind. I asked God to create in me a clean heart, search me, and remove those fears and doubts.

The next time that I saw Marvin, it was as if the clay had been removed from my eyes. My heart was full of joy, my eyes filled with tears, and I was proud to say that I was his and he was mine. I woke that Saturday morning crying as God continued to make me over, and I felt His presence in that hotel room while Marvin and his brother slept. I felt God opening up my heart to receive my breakthrough, I felt Him releasing all the doubts and fears, and I felt the love for Marvin that I once had emerging again. This time it was right, and we were on the right team.

When I asked Marvin why he had waited to get married, he simply replied, "I asked God for you a long time ago. I didn't know how, I didn't know when, I just knew it was going to happen." He stated that timing is everything. He was right—timing is everything, and God's time is not our time. He went on to explain the fisherman's concept to me. "I don't fish, but I've been told that the fisherman puts bait on his line and casts it into the water. If he leaves it out there long enough, the fish will nibble. Once the fish begins to nibble, you start to slowly reel the line in. Sometimes they will bite, and sometime they will just keep nibbling. Then when the line gets slack, you reel it in closer to take up the slack. Sometimes the fish will take all the bait, and you have to bait the hook again and throw it out again. If you keep on after a while, the fish will bite. When they bite, you must grab it and reel it in carefully so as not to lose the fish. A good fisherman has the patience to wait. Katrina, that's what I did with you. I waited patiently."

As children of God we must learn to wait patiently and trust God for our blessings. We are the heirs to a great promise, but we must learn to wait.

Chapter 13

It's Not About Me

To this John replied, "A man can receive only
what is given him from heaven. That joy is
mine and it is now complete, He must become
greater; I must become less."
—John 3: 27, 29-30 NIV

I had put off the inevitable long enough. I had run
long enough. It was now time to confess my calling and
walk in the steps that God had ordained. This would be
my final journey in this chapter of life. I was worried about
sharing the news with my family. My husband had known
for a while; we had discussed it in detail before we agreed
to marry. He knew that I would go when and where God
called, and he had agreed to get me there safely and back.
He was my number one supporter. He really was the man
that I had asked God for so many times.

My family took the news better than I expected. I had
talked to my godmother months before and knew that she
would settle my mother down. Mom had worked very hard
to convince me that God did not call women into ministry.

She had tried to prove that the Bible did not use women to lead. For many years I agreed with Mother. As a matter of fact, I was a lot like Paul in that I was the chief prosecutor of women in ministry. After all, that was what I had been taught my whole life. So what changed my mind? It was the personal relationship with God, His conversation with me and my conversation with Him. It was listening to His voice, seeing His vision for my life, and following His lead. I have heard all of the arguments about female ministry, but until it is realized that it is personal, people will continue to argue. Relationships with Christ are individual; one person does not know what and how God speaks to another. Furthermore, one person does not know the depth of the relationship with Christ. And God does not gossip, so He is not telling about the conversation. That is a good thing, so we can only go on a person's word.

I hoped that I would not get into a debate with Mom. I called Tae first as I began to open up and tell my family. He was excited and told me he was proud. He did a follow-up call on the next day to say thank you. When I asked for what, in his mild and meek attitude he just said, "For trusting me, Mom, even though we are far apart. I feel that we are so close together." There was a silence in his voice, and I knew at that moment that there was a lot more to be said and a lot more in his heart. He then said, "I love you, Mom."

I called Quenita a few days later. I thought she would be a tough cookie. "Well, Mom, I figured it was coming sooner or later, and if that's what makes you happy and what God told you to do, I guess you will have to do it." The next day, she sent a text message that said, "I will be there at your initial sermon to support you." When I called her that afternoon, she said, "Mommy, just don't change. I still want you to be my mommy. I don't want you to be one of those 'holier than thou' ministers. I want to still be able to talk to you and laugh with you. And Mommy, now I don't know what I believe."

My answer was, "I will always be your mommy, I will always love you, and just as God told me over a year ago to minister to women, I haven't changed, and I won't change." Finally, I told her, "As to what you believe, It has to be a personal thing. You must read and seek God for yourself. You must ask Him to guide and direct your life."

Next, I told my brother Freddy. I did not expect anything but support and a few questions from him. "When are you going to tell Mom? You mean I can't say anything about it to anyone?" Of course, I had also just told him that I had gotten married; that did not make matters better.

I told Dad, and of course, he did not say anything to Mom. I knew that Mom would be the one that would bring about all of her beliefs and past experiences. I wrote Mom a letter and told her that I had an appointment to profess who was the head and Lord of my life. She immediately went to my godmother. Well, I cannot tell you of their conversation; I just know that when I received her letter, all was well. As a matter of fact, it was as though things were better than well. She was happy and filled with joy—maybe not from my announcement, but there was a peace about her. We talked about it, and she said she had known for a while. It was the best talk that we had had in a while. Peace went all over me, and at that point, I released my all and all to God for use; everything that I had been trying to contain, I asked God to release and to use me like never before, and that He did. Remember, my friends, as you travel through life and in all that you do, it is never about us it is and will always be about Jesus, about the one who suffered and died for us all.

I will share with you inserts from my initial sermon, held on November 18, 2007.

Yes this is my initial sermon, but it is one more opportunity to praise the Lord, one more opportunity to say thank you, one more opportunity to share the good news, one more opportunity to tell someone of His goodness, and that is just what I intend to do.

If you have your road maps, turn with me to the book of John, and I will make reference to several verses in chapters 1 and 3. But I would like to read for your hearing John Chapter 1 verse 6-8, 23, and Chapter 3 verse 28-30.

From those passages of scripture I would like to briefly use for a subject:

Lessons from John the Baptist

Those that have heard me know that I don't appease to emotions; I believe that we have enough people playing on the emotions of Christians. It is our jobs to teach and feed God's people. In the twenty-first Chapter of John, verses 15-17, Jesus poses the question to Simon Peter three times and tells him all three times, "If you love me, feed my sheep." Thus, I believe that the Lord asking the same question of his followers today, 'Do you love me? Then feed my sheep.'

With that said, let's go on.

In our text today we find a unique account of John the Baptist. John the disciple is the author of this book, and he shares what some calls a bird's-eye view of Jesus.

He also shares information about John the Baptist that is not found in the other gospels, and while Luke does a very good job of discussing the early years of John the Baptist, Brother John picks up and discusses the end of John's ministry and the beginning of Christ's public ministry. And it is the ending of John's ministry that I want to concentrate on today, because John at the end of his ministry set an example for all Christians to follow today.

Lesson one: We are to bear witness and testify; John the Baptist was also known as the prophet and immediate forerunner of Jesus Christ. During two years of active ministry, John the Baptist prepared the people for the coming of Christ. He called on his hearers to repent of their sins, be baptized, amend their lives, and prepare for the coming of the kingship of God. He spoke of "one" greater than himself who was to come after. Today, we are no different; we as Christians are charged with witnessing and testifying about one who is coming. We are charged with carrying the word to those who are not saved about the coming of Christ. He is coming again. John the Baptist spoke of his first coming; as Christians today, we are charged with telling others that that same Jesus is coming again. We are to testify of his goodness. He has done something for all of us, and we should tell it. If he woke you this morning, you ought to tell it; we always pray, "Lord, you woke me up this morning with a portion of my health and strength, started me on my way, put food on my table, a roof over my head, and then won't tell a single soul." You don't need to tell God what he has done—he already knows—you need to go and testify and tell someone else. But we are so afraid of what someone might think, today's Christian won't even open their mouths to share the good news. Watch this: if a person wins the lottery, win at slots, win playing the boards, or wins by chance, there is not a problem getting on TV telling you, "I won one million dollars," but we can't tell a sinner how God put a loaf of bread on our table.

Well, let me move on to point two: The second lesson that we learn from John the Baptist is we are to know who we are and know our place. John the Baptist knew who he was and did not have a problem with it. Look at verse 20: "And he confessed, and denied not; but confessed I am not the Christ." Verse 23: "He said, I am the voice of one crying in the wilderness, make straight the way of the Lord." And finally, in Chapter 3 verse 28: "You yourselves bear me witness, that I said, I am not the Christ, but I am sent before him."

John the Baptist did not have a problem with who he was. If you would allow me to use my terminology, I can hear John the Baptist saying, "I am just a nobody, trying to tell everybody about somebody who can save anybody." I can imagine that John the Baptist was saying, "I'm out here in the wilderness preaching and teaching to anybody who will listen." This is a double lesson with a part A and B. Part A, then, is to understand this fully, we need to look at John the Baptist: he was born, raised, and lived in the wilderness, ate honey and locust. Why was that so? Some say that God had dwelled with His people after the Exodus, and it was a place of religious hope for

Israel. John called the people away from the comforts of their homes and cities and out into the wilderness, where they may meet God. Like John, if we are to get people to come to Christ, they must move out of the comforts of their homes, cities, and into the wilderness to meet God. "What are you talking about, Katrina?" Well, in our homes we have the radio, TV, telephones, DVD, CD, computers—everything that will prevent us from meeting God. There are too many distractions. In the city, there are too many lights, noises, sirens, sights, and sounds, but if we are to meet God, we must sometimes still away. Still away, go where you can hear the voice of Jesus whispering softly in your ear, get up early in the morning while the dew is still on the roses. Yes, sometimes we must go where the mosquitoes are biting to hear God's voice. Sometimes we just need a retreat away from it all. The best times that I have are walking around early in the morning or late at night, admiring God's creation; it is in the stillness that I feel closest to God.

Part B to this is to know your place. John knew his place—he knew who he was. He stated that he was just a voice crying in the wilderness; he repeated several times that he was not the Christ. He made sure that he let everyone know. In every scripture that I read, John repeated that he was not the Christ; he was just a forerunner. There was someone coming that was greater than he. A lesson that many need to learn. We are not the Christ; this thing is not about us. If you would again allow me to paraphrase, I can hear John saying, "You have this all wrong; I am not the one." You see, John had everyone questioning him, "Who are you?" John said, "I am just a nobody, trying to tell you something. He didn't get bigheaded because he had a crowd following him; he didn't get bigheaded because everyone was impressed by his preaching and teaching; he didn't change his way of dressing, way of talking, way of acting because he had a crowd following him. He was comfortable in his position. I want to take it a step further: when Jesus began to preach and attracted many followers, in fact many who were following John left him to follow Jesus. Some of John's followers resented this, but John told them, "This is as it should be. My mission is to proclaim the Christ. The groomsman, the bridegroom's friend, who makes the wedding arrangements for the bridegroom, he is not jealous of the bridegroom, No more am I of Jesus. In other words, I am not jealous of Jesus, I know my place, I am going to stay in my place. I am not Jesus, just making the way for him. Let me break it down: it's not about me, it's about Jesus." See, many of us need to take this lesson to heart. It's not about me, it's not about you—it's about Jesus and doing His work. It's about telling and showing somebody about His grace and mercy and how He saved you. Our job, like John's, is to point someone to the light, and it's a beautiful light. Shine all around us by day and by night—Jesus, the light of the world.

Finally, point three, and I am finished. I have told you that we are to bear witness and testify, we are to know who we are and know our place, and finally if Christ is to increase, we must decrease.

If Christ is to increase, we are to decrease. I have already told you that John was saying that it's not about him. Verse 8 says that he was not the light, he was sent to bear witness of the light. Further stated in Chapter 3 verse 30, John states that "he must increase, I must decrease." It is important to note that John described his own ministry as focused on Christ, saying that the sole purpose of his preaching and baptizing was that Christ should be made manifest—that is, that he should be made known to the people. We have far too many people who have this tangled up today. They want to increase while Jesus decreases. They want it to all be about them, not about Jesus. They want it to be about numbers in the church, not souls saved. They want it to be about the clothes they wear, not the clothes closet in the church. They want it to be about the car they drive, not the ones they wouldn't let get in the car. Yes, we have it messed up. It's not about us, it's about Jesus. We need to decrease while Jesus increases. John said,

I am not the Christ: I'm sent to announce him;

> I am the attendant: he is the bridegroom
> I listen and rejoice; he speaks
> I am enlightened; he is the light of life
> I must decrease; he must increase.

It's not about me, it's about Jesus. Thus we as Christians must say as John, "It's not about me, it's about Jesus and building his kingdom." This thing is larger than you and I. Don't ever think that it is not. If was only about me, I wouldn't be standing here. If it were about me, I would say, "Self, what are you thinking? Do you know what people are going to say about you? Self, what are you thinking, talking about preaching God's word? Self, you mean you are going to be on lockdown for the Lord? Self, you were having fun doing what you were doing; what do you mean you have decided to follow Jesus? Self, what were you thinking, saying, 'Lord, I will'?"

No, It's not about me, it's wasn't about John, it's not about the Jews or the Gentile. It's not about Baptist, Methodist, COGIC, Full Gospel, Pentecostal, or church without walls. It's not about the building—brick, block, or tin. It's not about preachers, stewards, or deacons; it's not about the trustees, the choir, or the ushers. It's not about mission or the meetings. It's not about what you've got, where you've been, or what you've done. It's about Jesus. It's about telling somebody about the light; it's about telling someone that one day a baby was born to a virgin Mary, walked the earth for thirty-three years, did no wrong, walked, and was an example for all to follow—was persecuted, lied on, marched from judgment hall to judgment hall all night, hung on a old rugged cross, beaten, bled, suffered, and died for your sins and mine, and rose again. And one day He is coming again. Yes, it is about him, and that is the perfect example that John left us. It is about Jesus and telling someone that he is coming back. I don't know about you, but not only am I going to tell someone, I'm waiting for that day for his return.

Author Biography

Katrina L. Roper-Smith is a native of Georgiana, Alabama. After having her first child at the age of sixteen and dropping out of high school, she did not give in to the challenges of life. At the age of twenty-seven, Katrina completed her BS from Troy University in Troy, Alabama. She continued her education by earning a master's from the University of Alabama and an educational specialist degree from Jacksonville State University, and she has completed all course work toward a doctoral degree from the University of Alabama.

Katrina has been an educator for the past eighteen years. Her experiences in the field are varied, however she has a passion for the underprivileged child and is deeply concerned about the social injustices that affect the students on campuses across America.

Katrina resides in Montgomery, Alabama, and currently serves as a minister and Christian education director at Shiloh AME Zion Church, Hope Hull, Alabama.

About the Book

I Think I Can, I Thought I Could, I Did . . . I Will: My Story details the life and challenges faced by a high school dropout and teen mother as she struggles to make life better for herself and her children. She realizes that her situation is not so different from other women across the country; many women are faced with challenges and are trapped in the maze of life. Unfortunately, women do not share their story with others. This book opens up the life of the author so that others may be healed and live productive lives in spite of their circumstances. It is only through the divine intervention of God that one can live a happy and productive life, however one must learn to say yes to the will of God.

King James Bible